The Economics of European Social Issues

by Roger LeRoy Miller
University of Washington

Harper & Row, Publishers

London New York Evanston San Francisco

First published 1975

Standard Book Number
06-318032-4 (cloth)
Standard Book Number
06-318027-8 (paper)

Set by Red Lion Setters,
Holborn, London

Designed by 'Millions'

Printed in Great Britain by
Biddles Ltd Guildford Surrey

Contents

Chapter 1

The Economics of Abortion

A small number of the major social issues of our time are purely economic; abortion is no exception. An economist has no answer to the question of whether life begins at conception or at quickening. Rather, he can only observe that because people have different beliefs as to when life begins, there will be some who want abortions and will be willing to pay for medical assistance. Abortion now becomes an economic problem. In a similar manner, most major social issues also become economic problems.

The performance of a pregnancy termination in many countries in the world has been and remains an illegal activity. For example, France has had an anti-abortion law on the books since the 1920s. These laws have at times been enforced with draconian severity. Under the Vichy régime during World War II, for example, a woman laundress convicted of performing twenty-six abortions was put to the guillotine. Anti-abortion laws are not nearly so strict in France and other countries some fifty years later; nonetheless, in many nations, women who undergo illegal abortions run a risk of prison sentences and fines that can sometimes exceed £1,000. In spite of the risk of prison sentences and fines, it is estimated that in France alone, over 1,000 abortions are performed every day! Many of these abortions are performed in unsanitary, back-street clinics by ill-trained, hygienically negligent abortionists. The risk of permanent crippling or death due to post-operation complications is not negligible. In fact, it has been estimated that hundreds of women in France die each year from post-abortion complications.

In April of 1971, France's *Le Nouvel Observateur* printed a list of 343 women, including actresses Jeanne Moreau, Catherine Deneuve, and authoresses Françoise Sagan and Simone de Beauvoir. Each of these 343 women publicly declared that: 'Je déclare avoir avorté'. Obviously, the social climate is ripe in countries such as France for a repeal or restructuring of all laws pertaining to pregnancy terminations. The results of such restructuring are well known in England and Wales, for after the passage of the Abortion Act, there was an increase of legally-performed abortions in Health Service hospitals that numbered over 100,000 in less than two years. It is interesting to contrast the economic conditions which prevail under the two circumstances, one in which abortions are illegal, and the other in which they are legal. First we look at the supply side of the picture: Who is willing to perform the illegal activity and at what price?

First we note that a licensed physician convicted of performing an illegal abortion generally faces not only criminal prosecution, but expulsion from his profession and a consequent lifetime loss of his medical licence and livelihood. In addition, he may be ostracized by a community which regards him as a criminal. In short, then, the cost to a doctor of such a criminal conviction is indeed immense. Nonetheless, illegal abortions are performed every day by many doctors who are commonly held in high regard. Those who prefer not to undertake these operations are sometimes willing to refer patients to other physicians who are prepared to take the associated risks. The fact is that the number of licensed doctors (and unlicensed ones, too) who are willing to take the risk of performing an abortion is directly proportional to the fee offered them. At a higher price, they are willing to supply more of their time to perform abortions, not only because at a higher price they are compensated more for the risk involved, but also because pregnancy terminations become relatively more profitable than their normal doctoring activities. Hence, we find not only that the total number of medical personnel willing to engage in illegal abortions rises as the price offered them rises, but also the amount of time that each of them will be willing to devote to such an activity also rises as the price rises. The relationship is a positive one.

The illegality of abortions has, of course, increased the costs of both supplying and obtaining information. Information is never free, even in legal activites, since it costs money to acquaint potential buyers with the location, price, and quality of a good or service. In the case of any illegal activity, the provision of information becomes, by necessity, more expensive. The illegal abortionist, for example, cannot publicize his price, location, or quality, for the more widely he lets his availability be known, the more he incurs risk of arrest. The high cost of information has its effects: women who seek an abortionist are not able to inform themselves of all the possibilities without spending large quantities of time and money in so doing.

Contrast these conditions with those where abortion is legal, quick and safe. Information is no more costly to disseminate or to obtain than for other medical specialities. Specialists can be listed in telephone directories, or, as occurs in some large cities in the United States today, in the classified advertisements of the daily newspapers. Anyone seeking a specialist can consult these sources or ask any physician for a referral.

Turning now from the supply side of abortion to the demand side, we note that the potential buyer of an illegal abortion faces a whole range of prices for the operation. In France, for example, a woman seeking a pregnancy termination can take a trip to England, Holland, or Switzerland, but, of course, there is an expense incurred here, both for the air fare and the time involved. At the other end of the scale, a French woman has the alternative of asking her local hairdresser where the closest 'cosmetic surgeon' is located. If we investigate the relative number of women in each of the above categories, we discover a definite pattern in which information costs and risks are important elements in each woman's decision. A relatively smaller number can afford or are willing to pay for the trip to another country; progressively more can and will pay the price at the lower end of the scale. Actually, many women feel that only the lowest price is within their reach.

It is hardly surprising that mortality from abortion appears to be inversely related to income. We have seen that a woman's inability to uncover reliable information can lead her to choose alternatives where she runs a higher risk of crippling, infection, and even death. All of the statistics from countries in which abortion is illegal corroborate this assertion. Morbidity and mortality from poorly performed abortions in unsanitary conditions mirrors the distribution of income.

We also note that when abortion is illegal, it carries the stigma of crime and, hence, many women are not willing to have the operation even if they do not wish to have a child. The removal of the stigma would result in a substantial increased demand, even at the same prices as before.

What can we predict in countries where anti-abortion laws are repealed? We predict that, among other things, the amount of post-abortion complications will fall, and the implicit price paid for abortions will also fall. As an aside, the number of women travelling abroad for abortions would also decline effectively to zero. That would mean, for example, that if anti-abortion laws were completely repealed in Germany, France and Belgium, there would be about 30,000 to 50,000 women from these countries a year who would not enter the United Kingdom to obtain pregnancy terminations.

The above argument could be construed as supporting evidence for anti-abortion law repeal. However, the above argument is only economic. It does not allow one to say definitively that the law under consideration is socially inappropriate. No economist can answer such a question because it involves moral and ethical issues as well. Presented above are the economic issues only. You will have to take into account the other factors for yourself.

Chapter 2

The Economics of Housing

The price of housing in Britain has been rising at phenomenal rates in the last half decade. It has not been unusual to see, for example, land values go up by 50 per cent in a twelve-month period. New houses in the London region in 1974 cost over 100 per cent more than they did at the end of the last decade. The British Government has, on occasion, repeatedly threatened (in a veiled manner, of course) to apply a fiscal axe to land profiteering. Similar, but perhaps not as dramatic, price increases for land and houses have been experienced in most major European countries. It is important, though, in analysing such price rises, to distinguish between a change in the relative price of housing as opposed to a change in the absolute price. The relative price of housing goes up if housing price increases exceed the average of all price increases in the economy or, otherwise stated, the rate of inflation. We know that house prices generally will go up with all other prices whenever there is a general inflation in any country. And since inflation seems to have become a way of life, in Europe, the United States, Latin America and everywhere else in the world, we can safely predict that the cost of housing will indeed increase for many years to come.

We expect the cost of actually building a house - the materials and labour - to also move along with the rate of inflation. Hence, the expectation of inflation is a cause of actual and potential landowners bidding up the price of land. That's exactly what has happened in Britain and throughout Europe. Now everyone anticipates that the last few years' high rates of inflation will more or less continue for many years. Site values have been bid up accordingly.

Two ways in which governments have attempted to significantly reduce the burden of rising housing costs have been, first, the granting of rent rebates; and, second, the provision of housing by public authorities. Generally, public housing in any country is provided at a price that is below its cost and is generally below the price that similar-quality housing can be purchased at in the private sector. Consequently, there are more people who wish to live in public housing than there is public housing available. A 'shortage' then exists. Those who are lucky enough to receive the subsidized housing benefit by the difference between what they pay and what they would have to pay in the private sector. Who pays for such a subsidy? Obviously taxpayers as a group. Are those who receive the subsidized living quarters made better off by the subsidy? Obviously they are. But we must note that they would be no worse off and, in general, would be better off if, instead of being provided with a subsidy in kind - i.e. housing - they were provided with the wherewithal to purchase housing. They could be no worse off, obviously, because they could use the subsidy in exactly the same way in which they now use it when they purchase public housing. They could be better off, however, if they used it in a way that might generate more benefit to them personally. It is difficult to understand why any particular government, whether it be in Britain, Scandinavia, or anywhere else, would decide that housing is something on which it must ensure that people spend the 'right' amount of income, for the option is always open of providing the subsidy in direct cash payments and letting the citizen, who is presumably in need, decide how that cash should be spent.

Another method that has been used to foster increased housing in Britain is the use of subsidized financing. This may sound like an ideal situation because it provides for a greater quantity of housing without involving the Government itself either in the direct activity of house-building or in the management of such activity. Nonetheless, a subsidized financing scheme is merely an indirect means of providing resources to a select group of people - i.e. homeowners - at a cost which is less than the cost that society must pay for that resource. It is interesting to note that in general, it is not the poorest income earners in any country who receive the benefits of such a subsidy.

One of the most ubiquitous means of supposedly protecting consumers of housing services from high prices has been and continues to be rent control. Control on rents in France dates back to the beginning of World War I. A major aspect of numerous British Labour Government economic packages to appease the masses is a freeze on rents. Sweden has for many years engaged in rent control in the city of Stockholm. Surprisingly, though, freezes on rents lead, at least in the long run, to just the opposite effect of what was desired. Rather than benefiting the public, rent controls hurt the public and lead to higher overall housing prices in the future.

When an investor buys an income-earning piece of property, such as a house to rent out or an apartment building or, for that matter, an office building, that investor will pay a price based on his projections of future profits to be made. The housing market in every city in the world is a highly competitive one, whether it be in London, Stockholm, Munich or Amsterdam. Since it is highly competitive, the rates of return or the profitability of investment in housing is generally no higher than the rate of return that can be earned on any other investment (at least not on the margin). Additional capital comes into any particular housing market whenever the profitability exceeds that of anywhere else in the economy. If, for example, more people suddenly decide to move from the countryside to the city, the future profitability of investing in housing in the city would rise and the future profitability of investing in housing outside the city would fall. Capital would slowly but surely shift into housing in the cities. The way that entrepreneurs would have realized that higher profits could be made by investing in city housing is because rents would have risen. Why? Because of the increased demand for housing in the city with a relatively fixed supply in the short run. The only thing that can happen is for rents to rise.

All of this analysis, of course, is predicated on the assumption that rents are indeed allowed to rise when the quantity of housing demanded exceeds the supplies available. And therein lies the problem with rent controls. If a government decides that the price that can be charged for rented housing must be set at a maximum below the price which would equilibrate the supplies with the demands, then there are no signals given to actual and potential investors to invest in more housing. The result is that the long run supply of housing is lower with rent control than without it. And since the long run supplies are lower, the price that is actually paid by the community for housing services will ultimately be higher. Hence we see the pernicious long-term effects of trying to freeze rents at levels below those which would prevail without governmental interference.

One must also realize that rent control may lead to a deterioration in the existing stock of housing. After all, one way for landlords to obtain a higher rate of return if they cannot charge a higher rent is to allow their properties to depreciate more rapidly than they would have otherwise. It is not unusual to find rent-controlled buildings in considerably more disrepair than non rent-controlled ones.

Some people obviously do benefit from rent controls. And they are the lucky ones who in fact were renting at the time that the controls were imposed. As the value of rental apartments and houses increases but the rents remain frozen, the existing tenants obtain a larger and larger transfer of wealth from the landlord. In situations where tenants in rent-controlled buildings can sublet their apartments, the transfer is obvious. In situations where they cannot, it is less so, but exists in any event.

What is important to realize in this whole discussion of rent controls is that whenever the price set for housing is below the price which would equate available supplies with actual demands, there will be a 'shortage'. Why do you think low-income families in rent-controlled accommodation in the city of Stockholm have waited in the official queue for apartments from five to eight years? Because the demand for rent-controlled apartments is greater than the supply. In such situations, there is room for negotiation between the owners of the rent-controlled apartments and the potential demand. One should not be surprised that high-income families can always get apartments through good 'contacts', or on the black market. It should not be surprising that various techniques are developed whereby those demanding rent-controlled housing devise methods by which they can induce landlords to let them the apartment rather than to someone else. This may be done by offering illegal 'money under the table'; this may be done by offering services to the landlord free of cost or by a million other ways. Quite understandably, landlords who must rent their apartments and houses at prices below what people are willing to pay find themselves in a position where they can discriminate much more than before. The landlord now has the opportunity to have tenants which suit his tastes to a tee. Of course, he would also have the opportunity in an uncontrolled situation, but it would cost him a lot more to exercise such discriminatory judgment.

If housing problems cannot be solved by rent control, how, then, is this social issue of the day to be resolved? Certainly the construction of public housing has been no panacea, as we mentioned above. In fact, public housing leads to the possibility of further types of discrimination. Catholics in Northern Ireland would certainly have had one less 'cause' had the institution of public housing for them been achieved. As a viable alternative, poor people in Northern Ireland, Britain or anywhere else, could be given housing vouchers which could only be spent for housing services. In this manner, there could never be any charge of discrimination against a housing authority, landlords would never be in situations where they had long queues waiting for apartments and the low-income recipients of these housing vouchers could determine how much additional income they wished to devote to the purchase of such an essential service.

Chapter 3

The Economics of the Population Explosion

Today there are many advocates of zero population growth. They put advertisements in newspapers and magazines which tell us of the horrors that await us in the future. Here's an example:

It was fun while it lasted but the party's almost over. Mother Earth has had enough. Every day of every year almost 350,000 babies are born on the Earth. That means a net increase of 70 million people each year, 70 million extra mouths to feed. The Earth can't handle it alone. It needs your help.
Bring the Earth back to the way it ought to be. Please consider all the good you can do. Please consider Zero Population Growth.

A disturbing advertisement, isn't it? An increase of 70 million people a year on the face of this Earth. There has got to be a limit somewhere and, in fact, someone figured out that the Earth presumably can accommodate 20 million times its present population. Living conditions, however, would be somewhat strange, as there would be 120 people per square metre enclosed in a 2,000-storey building covering the entire planet. And, at our present growth rate, it would take us less than 900 years to reach that far from enviable situation.

The zero population growth movement does not reflect the dawning of a totally new consciousness in world ecology. Indeed, the very groundwork for the movement's current *modus operandi* was laid by various colourful personalities from the past. The Reverend Thomas Robert Malthus was one such figure.

In 1798, the Rev. Malthus published an *Essay on the Principle of Population, as it Affects the Future Improvement of Society*. The uncomfortable and, indeed, depressing conclusion of that 50,000-word treatise was that 'population, when unchecked, goes on doubling every twenty-four years or increases in the geometric ratio', but, according to the Rev. Malthus, food production - more generally, the means of subsistence - only increases at an arithmetic ratio.

A few years later, in 1803, Malthus put out a second edition of his now infamous essay on population. Instead of talking about population doubling at a geometric ratio, he indicated that the human species was destined to poverty and a life of misery unless the rate of population growth was retarded by positive and preventive checks, such as late marriage, or no marriage at all, sexual abstinence, and moral restraint.

Even though Malthus preached moral restraint, he realized that 'hot passion leads to surplus souls and cold reason leads to sin'. And since he was of strong moral character, he appeared unimpressed by the low fertility of prostitutes for, as he put it, 'a promiscuous intercourse to such a degree as to prevent the birth of children seems to lower, in the most marked manner, the dignity of human nature'.

Malthus did, in fact, come up with a pretty good description of how things happened throughout Europe for many centuries before he wrote his essay. For example, there were recurrent periods of famine and pestilence, thus putting positive checks on the growth of population. There were also wars that had a similar effect.

What went wrong with Malthus' predictions so many years ago? Basically, he ignored the possibility of technological change. What he was looking at was a society in which technology was relatively fixed. For example, as the population grew in particularly favoured areas, the amount of land per man of course decreased, and not even the additional labour available could maintain the previous *per capita* food supply. For a while there was no cause for concern, since anyone who felt crowded out or deprived could simply move to the unsettled frontiers. It was on this basis that western Europe was colonized for many centuries. There came a time, however, when this situation changed, and the ubiquitous problem of diminishing returns set in. An additional peasant now either had to work the existing cultivated agricultural land more intensely than before, or move on to what proved to be much poorer land. Malthus predicted that diminishing returns had set in everywhere by the time he wrote his essay. Hence, the rate in growth in food production was bound to either remain constant or slow down and in any event, not keep up with the population growth.

What has happened, obviously, in the last several hundred years is that diminishing returns have been more than countered by increases in technology. We have out-smarted the Rev. Malthus. Modern Malthusians may have more sophisticated arguments, but their basic premise is the same: the Earth cannot support a growing population.

The rate of population growth is obviously a function of the rates of birth and death. While both have responded to economic changes, the triumphant decline of mortality in the past two centuries has accounted for much of the population growth throughout the Western world, and elsewhere. Anyone who thinks of a modern city as polluted would be quite appalled at the unsanitary conditions of its counterpart of even a century ago. We have seen that rising living standards, coupled with the application of improved sanitary and medical knowledge, has caused a drastic decline in death rates, particularly among infants, and this has become a potent factor in population levels.

We cannot, nonetheless, look to the mortality rate for any change in current population increases in the world. Rather, we must look to the birth rate as the way for controlling population size. In many countries of the world, the decision to have a child is now a deliberate one, and can be arrived at by a rational choice on the part of the family unit.

Even before the advent of modern birth-control techniques, couples still had ways to determine the number of children they would have. When marriage occurs at a later age in life, the birth rate would be lower. Celibacy, of course, is always an effective method of birth control, and it doesn't require modern techniques.

In any event, economists have found that fertility rates, or birth rates, can be explained by various economic variables. This is especially true in Western countries where birth control is widely practiced and relatively inexpensive. The more inexpensive birth-control methods become, the fewer unwanted babies there are likely to be.

If we treat children as an investment, the rate of return to that investment would most likely be an important determinant of how many children were desired. In most European countries today, however, to consider children as an investment is not to be taken seriously. We note, of course, that some parents do get a return on their investment later in life when their retirement is provided by their offspring. This is rare, though, as social insurance programmes and other retirement plans take care of parents throughout their old age.

It might be more appropriate to consider children as a consumption good. We would expect, therefore, that the normal determinants of the quantity demanded would prevail. What are these determinants? In the main, they are the price of the good and the income of the consumer. We would expect, in the absence of a change in people's tastes in favour of children rather than other consumption goods, that fertility would decline as an ever-growing proportion of Europeans become urbanized and are faced with the rising cost of bringing-up and educating their offspring. And this is precisely what is happening; fertility among Europeans and Americans, for example, is at the lowest level it has been in history. In the last few years in Britain, birth rates have fallen dramatically. While this may be a temporary phenomenon in Western countries, if it continues for some time we will quickly reach zero population growth without any help from modern-day Malthusians. In spite of this type of evidence, such groups as the British Population Panel continue to indicate that we're in for a population explosion somewhere in the future. While it is true that numerous under-developed countries are experiencing rapid rates of population increases, such is not the case in the Western world. In fact, some countries, such as France, have many times been worried about a reduction in total population rather than an increase. Why do you think that family allowances or subsidies have been so prevalent in places like France and Canada? Because parents respond to a relatively lower cost of raising children by having more of them. Obviously, the higher the family allowance per child, the greater will be the quantity of children produced.

The end of the world may be just around the corner, but it doesn't look as if it's going to occur because of a population crisis.

Chapter 4

The Economics of Future Energy Crises

As you probably remember, the Arabs put an oil embargo on oil exports to most of the major oil-consuming countries in 1973. All of a sudden, there was an energy crisis, or at least that's what we were told. All sorts of techniques were used to deal with this 'crisis'. Holland banned Sunday driving, for example. Ration schemes were instituted. Talks of more drastic measures were in the air.

In order to understand the next energy crisis, it is helpful to see what happened during 1973-1974.

There's been a world oil cartel around for a long time. But you never heard of it before the 1970s, did you? The reason you never heard of it was that, until recently, it wasn't very effective. A cartel is only effective if it can restrict production; otherwise, it has no effect whatsoever. The Persian Gulf oil-producing countries wanted to extract monopoly profits out of their black gold a long time ago. Unfortunately, there were always chiselers on any agreement. After all, the incentive to chisel is always there. That's the nature of the economic beast, whether he be at home or abroad. Moreover, the world's oil supply doesn't all reside under the sands of the Middle East. A lot of it is found in Africa and elsewhere. But even if that were not the case, the analysis would still hold. The only way to extract monopoly profits is to have a monopoly, and the only way you can have a monopoly is by making sure that nobody cheats on a cartel agreement. Once this is done, it follows that each member of the cartel can be made to cut back the supplies of his output. This is the only way of ensuring that the price is kept up simply because the same quantity of anything (just about) cannot be sold at a higher price if nothing else changes.

Getting back to the world cartel. In 1960, an oil cartel - the Organization of Petroleum Exporting Countries (OPEC) - was established: it included Abu Dhabi, Algeria, Indonesia, Iran, Iraq, Kuwait, Libya, Nigeria, Qatar, Saudi Arabia and Venezuela. (Ecuador has recently joined the Organization.) When it came into existence, its purpose was obviously to maximize the benefits from owning oil for its members. It couldn't do much during the sixties because there seemed to be an ever-expanding supply that was keeping ahead of demand. As demand grew, new discoveries expanded supply so fast that well-head prices for crude oil actually fell slightly from 1960 to 1970. Then in 1970 and 1971, the rate of growth of the demand actually slowed down. So it seems improbable that the cartel would have really got going at that time. But it did, and in part its new power was caused by some unwise and unfounded interventions on the part of Western governments. Representatives of all importing nations were convened in Paris in 1970 after Libya and the Persian Gulf countries had already raised crude-oil prices fairly dramatically in a very short period of time. It appears that the United States Government thought this type of hostile behaviour indicated a threat of an oil embargo: accordingly it convinced other countries at the Paris meeting that it was in everyone's best interests to agree to the price rises.

The Persian Gulf nations saw a good thing coming. Western nations' compliance resulted in the threat of an embargo unless prices were increased again. What did the Western countries do? Their representatives attended the Tehran and Tripoli conferences where agreements were signed in 1971 which granted all exporting oil countries in OPEC huge increases in their price per barrel of crude oil. These agreements were signed by all OPEC members and by many oil companies. In essence, however, it was the governments of the importing countries who were signing those agreements.

The governments of European countries ignored some basic economics. You can't raise prices unless you have a monopoly. You can't have an effective cartel unless it has got some way of preventing people who are in the cartel from cheating. All the importing nations had to do when they met together in Paris was to tell OPEC 'no go', instead of ratifying the suggested price increases. An agreement among the importing nations could have countered any OPEC monopoly power. For example, one suggestion that has been put forth is that importing countries can make selling agreements among the various companies. In other words, all oil companies agree to sell crude oil to any other company which OPEC members might shut down. The crude oil is sold to the shut-down company at cost plus taxes. This way, shutting down any particular oil company within the OPEC region would not affect to any great extent world oil supplies. In this way, OPEC would know that it couldn't pressure importing countries and that it did not have much monopoly power. In fact, we see this in the admission of the Shah of Iran who said in 1971: 'If the oil-producing countries suffer even the slightest defeat, it would be the death-knell for OPEC, and from then on the countries would no longer have had the courage to get together.' Unfortunately, the importing countries gave in without so much as a fist-fight.

Let's look at this situation a little more carefully. Did OPEC need the 1973 Arab-Israeli war to cut off production and raise prices? In a way it did, but not for the reasons you might think. It was planning to raise prices anyway, and of course the only way it could keep those prices up was to restrict the output of the various member countries. As output is restricted more and more, prices rise higher and higher; however, the incentive to cheat becomes unbearable. Sooner or later such an arrangement has to fail. This time it was Iran who broke the agreement almost from the very beginning and was supplying oil at the going price to whoever would pay for it.

You have to realize that as the price rises, other countries who are not members of the cartel have an incentive to increase shipments. But as those shipments increase, it takes further reductions in the production of the OPEC companies to keep up the price. Sooner or later something has to give, and something of course has to give when you consider that it costs at most less than a dollar, and perhaps not much more than 10 to 40 cents, to produce a barrel of crude oil in the Middle East. Compare that to the $4, $5, $8, $9, $10 or whatever price that was being charged for Arab oil after the war. When what you're selling yields you ten times its cost in revenues, that's a pretty high profit, and one you would certainly like to get into expanding production, right? But all along the cartel is telling you to cut back production so as to keep the price up. The 1973 Arab-Israeli war turned out to be an excuse to do what OPEC was going to do anyway. What it did was provide the glue to hold the cartel intact; the cheats had a harder time cheating. The oil industry has thought all along, and continues to think, that the OPEC cartel will eventually collapse because that glue has got to crack sometime. Most knowledgable oil men give the cartel no more than three years.

Now you know why we're bothering to get oil out of Alaska and the North Sea even though it's costing considerably more than it costs to bring it out of the Arabian desert - because the West submitted to the OPEC cartel, meaning that world oil prices are high enough to make this very expensive Alaskan and North Sea oil worth getting. From a worldwide efficiency basis, it is ridiculous to spend the resources to bring that Alaskan and North Sea oil into the world today. The West should first be using up that really cheap oil in the Middle East. But so long as OPEC remains firm, that cheap oil is going to be selling at ten to twenty times its cost. OPEC pricing and production restricting tactics, however, will ultimately lead to its demise. Soon new sources of oil and other energy sources will be supplying more and more fuel in response to these high prices. Then there's going to be a cheat, OPEC will break down, and the world price of oil will plummet. You can bet on that, unless human nature has changed in the last year and cheating no longer occurs.

It must not be forgotten that the West is extracting a very small percentage every year of total proven world reserves. The latest estimate is that we're taking out less than 3 per cent, which isn't much. Now of course, even at 3 per cent a year, with a fixed amount of reserves we'd eventually run out. A funny thing, though, happened on the way to the forum. Proven reserves are greater today than they were in 1935, even though we've consumed much more oil than we ever thought we would. But how could this be, you might ask. Easy. Proven reserves mean just that - reserves known and proven and available at current market prices for oil. It has been discovered that, to date, as the price goes up, more reserves are found. As technology changes, more reserves become commercially viable because they can be profitably taken out of the ground. Of course, that still doesn't mean that the WEst has enough oil to last from here to eternity. At any rate of use, no matter how small, we will eventually run out if Nature isn't forming any new oil. But that's just a truism, no more relevant than observing that inflation means rising prices.

At some time in the future, Arabs may decide to increase the price of oil exported to Europe again. And if that happens, another so-called energy crisis will prevail unless European governments do not repeat the same follies they engaged in in 1973 and 1974. One country that didn't have any problem was West Germany, and the reason it didn't have any problem was because during the Arab oil embargo, it allowed oil prices to rise, thus diverting foreign oil away from countries with price controls, such as Britain, Sweden and Italy. To be sure, panic drove prices way up for a couple of months during the 'crisis', but by the spring of 1974, petroleum in Germany was only 10 per cent more costly than it had been before the crisis.

It has to be remembered that when there is a precipitous reduction in the supply of any good that is in demand, there will be more demand than available supplies at the prices that prevailed before. If prices are not allowed to rise, shortages will occur, a crisis will develop. Rationing does nothing to eliminate that shortage. It is merely a cumbersome method by which available supplies are distributed to consumers at prices below those which would prevail without controls. The lucky recipients of the rationed oil product supplies are treated to a redistribution of wealth from other members of society. If that's why you want to ration petroleum then you may be in favour of such government activity. But if you believe that rationing can solve a shortage, you are sadly mistaken. In fact, rationing (that is only necessary when there are price controls) results in an increased shortage, and that for two reasons: first of all, those who obtain the rationed amounts of petroleum products at artificially low prices have little incentive to conserve and, secondly, producers who cannot benefit from higher prices have little incentive to expand production.

The rationing that some European countries engaged in in 1973 and 1974 did not solve the energy crisis at that time. What solved the so-called crisis was the fact that oil was entering Europe in spite of the embargo because the incentives for cheating on the OPEC agreement were tremendous. And, of course, by the spring of 1974, the embargo was lifted. The same economic principles which predict that agreements such as the one entered into by OPEC will ultimately fail can be used to predict that any time a temporary reduction in the supply of petroleum occurs, shortages will prevail unless the price is allowed to equate the new supply with demand.

Chapter 5

The Economics of Prostitution

In 1945, a French politician - one Mme Marthe Richards - demanded the closing of all Paris brothels. She claimed that the 178 licensed houses, 600 prostitute-serving hotels, 100,000 pimps, and 6,600 ladies of the night were 'undermining Parisian morals and health'. Moreover, she estimated that the closing of brothels would make available 6,000 rooms for students and those bombed out of their homes during the war.

The Municipal Council of Paris, impressed by her statistics, gave the brothels three months to shut down. The effects have been far-reaching, to say the least, and apparently have not proved too satisfactory for some participants, because there are rumours that a campaign might be shaping-up in France to restore the legality of the world's oldest profession. Although the product differs considerably, the economic analysis of prostitution is similar to that of abortion with, of course, a few added twists.

The service that prostitutes offer for sale has, like all others, two dimensions: quantity and quality. In some sense, these are inter-related; quantity can be increased by lowering quality. The quality of the service is, among other things, a function of: (1) experience; (2) innate characteristics of the provider of the service, such as looks and intelligence; and (3) current operating expenditures, such as how much money is spent on appearance, surroundings, and health. To be sure, substitution is possible among these three aspects of quality. Perhaps the same quality can be achieved either by being born beautiful or by spending effort and money on make-up and clothes. Some ladies of the night are able to compensate for poor looks by dressing well. For instance, some ladies are able to substitute clothes for natural physical endowments.

For many who utilise the services of a prostitute, the health aspect of quality is of utmost importance. The decision to make prostitution illegal in France had notable consequences on the probability of some clients' contracting venereal disease.

When prostitution was legal, there were numerous business establishments whose sole purpose in life was offering prostitutes' services. They could afford to advertise without risk. Because clients could easily compare prices and qualities, information was relatively cheap. If it became common knowledge that the employees of one house spread venereal disease to their customers, that firm would either have to lower its prices drastically or suffer a drop in clientele.

Even though cheap information made it inadvisable for any of these firms to employ unhealthy employees (since their clients would go elsewhere), the French Government made doubly sure that venereal disease was kept at a minimum by requiring weekly medical inspections. Most prostitutes worked in establishments, and it was relatively easy to check all of them; disease was rare among prostitutes before 1947. The reader can easily draw the analogy between the cases of legalized prostitution and legalized abortions.

When prostitution was legal, suppliers of this service charged their opportunity cost, with no risk factor added in, since no threat of imprisonment or fines existed. Demand for the services did not involve the investment of large amounts of resources (time and effort) and obtaining information that would help avoid the risk of a poor-quality product, such as represented by the threat of disease.

What has happened in France since 1947? There are no more legal houses of prostitution, and the girls, for the most part, have taken to the streets. The cost of doing business has increased. Street-walkers must avoid detection and arrest either by cleverness or by paying off *les flics.* Some girls must stay outside more than before, adding a cost of discomfort. Also, they no longer benefit from economies of scale that previously kept down the cost of accessories to their trade, such as attractive setting and atmosphere.

At the same wages as before, fewer prostitutes were willing to stay in the profession after 1947. On the demand side, clients can no longer be so confident about the quality of the product, because open competition among legal houses has been removed. Previously, any house with a bad reputation suffered; now, individual prostitutes can more easily lower quantity and still obtain clients, for information has become much more difficult to obtain. Finally, there are no longer governmental medical inspections.

Predictably, as information about quality has become more expensive, only the wealthy citizen has been able to afford the cost of seeking out the healthy prostitutes, while the poor citizen has contracted venereal disease. If a poor woman suffers from a bad abortion, the rest of society bears little of the cost. But if a dock worker contracts venereal disease, he is not alone in bearing the cost; other members of society must also pay, because he can spread the disease to others. This problem may explain in part why one would expect a fervour about legalizing prostitution in countries where it is still illegal.

France, of course, has not been the only country to ban prostitution; the United States, for example, for the most part, suppresses prostitution as vigorously as any other place in the world. It is not surprising that venereal disease rates in the United States have hit new highs every month and have become a major public health problem.

And if the illegality of prostitution and the consequent increased expenses are not enough, today's prostitutes are facing a smaller demand than in the past because of the 'new morality'. When the supply of free love increases, the demand for more costly forms of sexual release falls. Free love and non-free love are substitutes for some people. Therefore, people buy more of the relatively cheaper commodity.

While it may be true that nothing is indeed free and in fact the true cost of free love may be rather high, the relative supplies of the two substitutable commodities are drastically changing. While it is certainly true that free love will never completely replace the services rendered for pay, ladies of the night are experiencing a lower rate of return than they would had morals stayed high.

Chapter 6

The Economics of Euphoria

In many European countries today, marijuana is illegal; so are hashish, mescaline, di-methyltryptamine, psilocybin, and tetra-hydrocannabinol. Their illegality, like the illegality of abortions, does not, of course, prevent their use. It does, however, add certain peculiar characteristics to their production, distribution, and usage, characteristics similar to the production and sale of abortions.

In most European countries, mild halocinogens are in fact illegal. The British Misuse of Drugs Act, for example classifies *cannabis sativa*, along with amphetamines and codein, as a B drug, for which unlawful possession attracts a maximum penalty on indictment of five years' imprisonment. On the other hand, the maximum penalty for supplying or intending to supply marijuana is fourteen years' imprisonment. It is also well known in Europe that an extremely well organized, illegal trafficking in heavier drugs, such as heroin, is concentrated in such areas as southern France - more specifically, Marseilles. The Union Corse, an organization that originated in Corsica, is now centred in that city. It apparently dominates worldwide traffic in hard narcótics, particularly the supply and processing of the heroin that flows to North America through France from South America and South-East Asia.

The production, processing, distribution and consumption of illegal drugs is big business on a worldwide basis. We can learn a few things about the characteristics of this business by examining a unique and unforgettable experience in the history of the world - the prohibition against the production, distribution, and consumption of alcoholic beverages in the United States during the 1920s.

On 16 January 1920, the Eighteenth Amendment to the Constitution of the United States became effective. It prohibited

'... the manufacture, sale, or transportation of intoxicating liquors within, the importation thereof into, or the exportation thereof from the United States ... for beverage purposes ... .' The Volstead Act, passed in 1919, forbade the purchase, possession, and use of intoxicating liquors.

The results were impressive, but could have been predicted by any economist. Since the legal supply of liquor and wine fell to practically zero* while much of the public continued to demand the commodity, substitutes were quickly provided. Supplies of illegal liquor and wine flowed into the market. Increasing quantities of whiskey clandestinely found their way across the border from Canada, where its production was legal.

Of course, fewer entrepreneurs were now willing to provide the American public with liquor. Why? Mainly because the cost of doing business suddenly increased. Any potential speakeasy operator had to take into account a high risk of being gaoled or fined or both. He also faced increased costs of operating his bar, for usual business matters had to be carried on in a surreptitious — i.e. more costly — way. Moreover, the speakeasy operator had to face the inevitable encounter with the Mafia. He could look forward to paying-off organized crime in addition to the local police. Payments to the former reduced the possibility of cement shoes and the East River. Payments to the latter reduced the probability of landing in jail.

In general, Prohibition decreased the amount of alcoholic beverages that entrepreneurs were willing to provide at the same price as before. If a bottle of one's favorite Scotch were available

*The exception was wine intended for religious purposes. Production of so-called sacramental wine increased by 800,000 gallons in the two years following ratification of the Eighteenth Amendment, leading to the interesting speculation whether Prohibition somehow made Americans suddenly more religious.

for $3.00 in 1919, it either would have cost more in 1920 or the same bottle would have been filled with a lower-quality product.

Whiskey lovers faced another problem during Prohibition: they could no longer search newspaper advertisements and billboards to find the best buys in bourbon. Information had also gone underground, and even learning about quality and price had suddenly become more costly. When goods are legal, they can be trademarked for identification. The trademark cannot be copied, and the Courts protect it. With such easily identified goods, consumers can be made aware of each product's quality and price. If their use of a product does not jibe with their anticipations, they can quit buying the 'bad' product. It thus becomes apparent why some unfortunate imbibers were being blinded or killed by the effects of bad whiskey. There was no way to tell quality. The risk of something far more serious than a hangover became very real.

The new whiskey-drinking costs were outweighed, for some, by the joys of the speakeasy atmosphere. But other more ethical drinkers were deterred from consuming as much liquor as they had before 1920, even had it been obtainable at the same price as before.

The impact of Prohibition, like the impact of abortion bans, favoured the rich at the expense of the poor. The high-income drinker was less discomfited at having to pay more for his brand of whiskey. He ran little risk of being blinded. The high-price tag and the cost of obtaining information about quality and supply could not separate him from his bourbon.

Some lower-income imbibers had probably been paying just about their limit for whiskey of acceptable quality before Prohibition. The sudden rise in costs left them facing the alternative of either doing without or settling for less - bootleg booze and bathtub gin. The occurrence of injury, sickness, and death from contaminated whiskey directly mirrored the distribution of income.

What happened during Prohibition is happening now with drugs. Illegal drugs, like bootleg bourbon, have relatively high costs and high risks in their manufacture, distribution, sale, and consumption. The wealthy user is still able to buy quality, and may even pay intermediaries to do his shopping around; the middle-income user ends up getting inferior drugs. Yet there is a difference between the two periods. Some poor people who are high-consumption users - the 'heads' - often obtain the better-quality euphorics, and frequently at prices below those paid by others. The reason involves a mixture of economics and sociology. First, such people would not be poor if they were not working at such low-paying jobs (if they are working at all). Therefore, when they spend time away from the job, not much income is lost and economists say that the opportunity costs of their not working are low compared to those people with higher-paying jobs who must sacrifice more earnings when they choose not to work. The poor user merely responds to his low opportunity cost when he spends more time seeking out the best buys in the drugs he urgently wants. This was true during Prohibition with booze, but there was no large sociological class now known as 'heads' who were devoted to a whiskey 'cult'.

When a middle-income drug user spends time seeking out information about which drugs to buy and where to find them, he is confronted with higher costs for his time away from work. Potential jailing is a greater deterrent both in opportunity costs and in psychic and emotional costs. Since he is probably unable or unwilling to pay some intermediary to do his searching for him (as the rich user would do), he ends up with drugs of a quality that would be scorned by many low-income 'heads'.

Relatively well-off European women living in countries that have anti-abortion laws fly off or take a train to some other country to have a legal abortion performed. Why do rich users not fly overseas to obtain and use their drugs in Nepal, for example, where high-quality marijuana can be purchased for about ½-1p per ounce? The price at home might run as high as £15 for the same quality and quantity. The relative price of Nepalese marijuana is thus 1/2,000 that of the European product. Or is it? When we consider the total cost, we see that we must include round-trip air fare to Nepal, plus the opportunity cost of the flight time (minus any value placed on seeing that exotic country). The relative price of one ounce of legal Nepalese marijuana now becomes more like £0.08 + £333 − £16, or twenty times the illegal price in Europe.

Up to now, we have been dealing mainly with people who want to buy illegal drugs. Now, we want to find out what determines the quantity people are willing to sell at various prices. Drug suppliers parallel whiskey suppliers during Prohibition. Illegal manufacture and distribution of most drugs poses a large risk to suppliers. The risk is higher the greater the probability of detection and conviction, and the greater the potential gaol sentence and/or fine. Costs of doing business include measures to assure secrecy and avoid detection, pay-offs to organized crime (for certain drugs not easily manufactured, like heroin), and potential pay-offs to the police.

What would happen if marijuana were legalized? Should we expect a general state of euphoria? Sellers would be able to supply quantities at lower prices than before because the costs of doing business would fall. No risks would be involved, no requirement for pay-offs to organized crime, no high cost of maintaining secrecy in production and distribution. The price of many drugs would eventually fall to a level just covering the lower costs of legal production and distribution.

Legalization would also reduce the costs of disseminating and obtaining information about supplies through advertising. Competition among sellers and increased information available to buyers would combine to raise the quality of the product.

When there is unrestrained competition among sellers of a legal product, it is difficult for relatively inferior products to exist side-by-side with better ones unless the price of the poorer product is sufficiently lower. Sellers of the superior product will inform the buying public of the anomaly. Since the product is legal, the relatively unrestricted flow of information will ensure that some buyers will refuse to purchase the high-priced, low-quality drugs.

For buyers, legalization would also end the threat of detection, conviction and gaol. Higher overall quality would reduce the risk of bad side-effects from improperly-prepared drugs. Both cost reductions would lead consumers to demand a larger quantity at the same prices which had prevailed before legalization.

Prices might rise immediately after legalization. The increase in demand might exceed the increase in supply, causing temporarily higher prices, but consumers could obtain as much of the now-legal product as they want at those prices. In the long run, however, prices would probably fall to a level just covering the costs of production, distribution, and normal profit - which would certainly be lower than the price paid today.

If drugs were legalized and prices dropped, alcohol would become relatively more expensive. Would people drink less and smoke pot more? The answer hinges on an 'if'. If marijuana is a substitute for alcohol, this might well happen. However, if the two are complementary, increased use of marijuana would lead to increased use of alcohol. Current tastes suggest that wine and 'weed' go together, but bourbon and 'grass' do not 'sit well'.

Chapter 7

The Economics of Health Care

Nationalized health care, such as by the British National Health Service is supposed in principle to lead to improved services at lower costs. In reality, however, as Britain has painfully learned, a nationalized system can also lead to dissatisfied doctors, runaway costs, and over-utilised services. An issue of *Medical World News* a few years ago reported that 'half of Britain's medical graduates are expatriots'. The reason is not hard to find - huge hospital workloads, low pay, and long hours. In fact, the hours of a doctor in Britain demanded by his or her government exceed those in any other field, just about. In fact, the earnings of an accountant in England are probably double those of a general practitioner. The kind physician who agrees to make a house call between 12.00 midnight and 7.00 am earns less than £3 for his efforts.

The 10,000 or so general practitioners that are employed by the British Government are really 'private contractors'. The G.P. is paid a set fee for each patient on his panel. Now, of course, these doctors have to be paid, as do hospital personnel and all the other persons associated with the National Health Service. The Exchequer is the department which ends up footing the bill - i.e. the taxpayers pay almost the full amount. Medical care in Britain is 'free' except for a nominal charge on prescriptions, with some other fees for things like spectacles. You'll notice that the word 'free' was put in quotes. The reason it was put in quotes is because few things in this world, or any that we know of, are free. It may be free to the user, but it can never be free to society. Participants in the National Health Service in the United Kingdom obtain medical care at usually a zero price, but the cost to them, taken as a whole, is indeed the total cost of the system; they merely pay for it through taxes. Herein lies one of the reasons that the British system finds itself with over-utilised services.

While it may be thought that medical care is 'essential' or a 'necessity', people respond to changes in the price of medical care just as they respond to changes in the price of any other good or service they purchase. When the price of medical care in Britain fell to zero after the institution of socialized medicine, the quantity demanded jumped drastically. That would be true for just about any other product or service in any economy which was offered to consumers at an artificially low or, as in this case, zero price. As an aside, when the public knows it can obtain medical services at no additional cost individually, there is less incentive for each individual to prevent illness and disease. After all, the cost of medical repairs is zero. An analogy can be drawn between medical services and motor-car services. What if there were nationalized motor-car repair in a country? Would there not be less incentive for each individual motor-car owner to take preventive care of his vehicle? Obviously, there would be less incentive and there would be more demands made on the nationalized repair service.

There's also another reason that the National Health Service suffers from over-utilised facilities. That reason involved the reduction in the incentive for anybody to build new hospitals during the first fifteen years of socialized medicine in Britain. Hospitals are now more obsolete than they would have been without the National Health Service. In an alternative situation where there is no nationalization of the health service but, rather, a private system exists with or without health insurance, then, as more people demand more and better medical care, so more hospitals are built to satisfy that demand. This is exactly what has happened - e.g. in the United States where for most of its history, almost all medical services have been provided privately. The percentage of total national income being spent on medical services has increased from practically nothing at the start of that country to almost 8 per cent today. With this increased demand for medical services has come an increase in the supply of medical facilities. Such has obviously not been the case in Britain.

It is also certainly true that waiting lists have not been shortened. It looks as though 'free' government services have bred discontent in a public with rising expectations. According to some observers of the British scene, many people feel they get better, faster attention by paying as private patients. In fact, we know that that must be true because private specialists' practice in Britain has been growing for a number of years now. Of course, the British Government randomly puts out White Papers on private practice and National Health Service hospitals, attempting to keep the growth of such practice down. Nobody likes competition, particularly a government. It is interesting to note that the Government in Britain so far has not given many concessions to private practice at all. In most cases, private patients have to pay the full cost of the hospital bed, even though they have already paid for at least part of it by way of taxes and social security.

This is no different than, for example, the situation with regard to private versus state schools in nations where taxes must be paid to support a state-school system even if one does not wish one's children to attend such an institution. For example, in the United States where this is the case, there are still a large number of private schools. Parents who send their children to those private schools must pay twice, once in tuition to the school itself and once again to the Government in the form of taxes for state education, which of course these parents do not benefit from. We must conclude that on both counts - the people seeking private health services in Britain and for parents seeking private school services in America - the benefits from private service still outweigh the double costs that must be paid.

What is important in this whole discussion is not the fact that

British medical services have been nationalized, but that a system in which prices are used to indicate the relative social costs of the services provided were abolished in favour of 'free' health care that was financed almost 100 per cent by taxation. Other nationalized industries in Britain and elsewhere have not suffered a similar fate. Electricity, coal, gas, to name only a few, are nationalized in many countries but nonetheless increasingly charge economic prices and respond to changing consumer demands. There were, to be sure, many arguments in favour of the abolition of prices in the national health system. The arguments, as we shall see, are quite weak.

One of them involves the idea that the abolition of prices will not only ensure the best standard of service for all but also ensure that low-income citizens will get adequate medical care. In the first place, we find that the evidence shows that systems without prices do not lead to higher quality but, rather, to lower quality. In the second place, it is not necessary to abolish the pricing system in order to ensure that low-income people can get adequate medical care. We can provide low-income people with higher incomes via direct welfare payments or, as in the case with housing mentioned in Chapter 2, we could provide them with medical care 'vouchers' which could only be used for medical treatment.

Some of the other arguments used to support the lack of prices in the British national health system involve the desire to remove the 'financial barrier between doctor and patient and also simultaneously remove the"tax" on sickness'. In the first case, the 'financial barrier' exists between any consumer of any good and any supplier of any good, whether it be medical care, food, clothing, or housing. These items are just as essential to life as medical care and, therefore, if this argument were to be taken seriously, one would nationalize the entire housing, clothing, and food industries and provide all of these services at a zero price to taxpayers. With respect to the 'tax on sickness' argument, we could in the same vein talk about the price of food as a 'tax on hunger', or the price of housing as a 'tax on exposure'. We could do this on every item that anybody purchases for whatever reason, if we wanted to extend the argument to its logical absurd end.

As we mentioned above, one of the reasons that there are so few doctors in England that were born in England is because the relative rates of pay for doctors in the nationalized system are quite low. It is not surprising that a British-trained physician has an incentive to go to other countries, such as the United States where their incomes would be much higher than in the British Isles. One of the reasons that incomes are so high for doctors in the United States is because physicians there are members of one of the strongest, if not *the* strongest, unions in that nation. They have effectively restricted entry into that profession for many years now by establishing over-rigorous criteria for medical schools and punishing any medical school which allows 'too many' medical students in any one year. In essence, doctors in the United States have practiced under a monopoly shield for the last half-century, and their incomes show it. Doctors throughout Europe have, but apparently to a much less successful degree, attempted to foster the same type of monopoly atmosphere.

While it is certainly true that the Treaty of Rome gives professionals the right to practice in the community where they please, it is not all that easy for a private doctor in Milan to set up a new practice in Paris. A German obstetrician could not deliver children in Dublin without any questions asked. There is obviously an incentive for each nation's doctors to band together to prevent such free movement of physicians within European countries. Holland, for instance, is quite a bit ahead of Britain in terms of the lifetime earning prospects for physicians. The attraction for a British-trained physician to move to Holland is obviously a real one for the newly licensed M.D. And it can be expected that the British Medical Association (BMA) would fight for its integrity and independence from nations across the channel.

It's also not hard to understand why the Common Market countries have decided at the behest of physicians' interest to specify a rather high standard to allow any doctor to move from one nation to another. The basis of medical education has been defined as 5,500 hours of instruction spread over six university years. The amount of problems of this nature that will be faced in the Common Market countries in years to come will probably be legion and sometimes insurmountable. But the rationale behind such behaviour is perfectly economic: any doctor in any country who thinks that he will be hurt by competition from foreign doctors entering his profession will be against the free movement of physicians from one country to another.

When one compares the private system in the United States, for example, along with its almost complete monopolization of the supply of doctors, with the nationalized system in Britain, it is certainly not obvious which system is better for the average citizen. However, in the former case, one obvious improvement would involve the elimination of the monopoly status of the American Medical Association (AMA). In the latter case, one improvement would be the reinstitution of a pricing system in the nationalized system so that consumers of medical services would know the true social cost of the services they were buying.

Chapter 8

The Economics of a Common Farm Policy

One of the few things that has worked in the EEC has been its common agricultural policy (CAP). Basically, the CAP supports the prices of most European farm products at common levels well above what would normally prevail without intervention. And except for certain periods during the last few years, the supported prices in the EEC countries have been considerably higher than in Britain and in the rest of the world. In order to understand the full nature of the CAP and its effects on farmers and consumers alike, let's look at the market for agricultural commodities prior to the advent of the EEC's farm policies.

Let's look at a competitive market where a large number of farmers are supplying a particular commodity - say, wheat. The sum of the quantities that individual farmers supply at various prices will make up the aggregate supply of that commodity. Each farmer in this situation only supplies quite a small part of the total quantity of wheat. He cannot, therefore, influence the price of this product. For if he raised his price, anyone wishing to buy wheat could easily buy it from someone else at the going (equilibrium) price. He would never want to sell it at less than the going price for he would be making less money than possible. Hence every unit of output of an individual farmer sells for exactly the same price. The price received for the last (marginal) unit sold is exactly the same as that received for all the rest.

The farmer, whether he be French, English, Dutch or German, will produce wheat up to the point where if he produced one unit more, its production costs would be greater than the price received. At higher prices, however, farmers can and will incur higher costs for additional units produced and still make a profit. Thus, we see that at higher prices, all farmers collectively will produce more. No farmer will stop producing until he stops making a profit. That is to say, each farmer will end-up selling wheat at the going price which will equal his cost of production plus a normal profit.

Now the price at which any individual farmer can sell his wheat depends on how people feel about buying it and that, of course, depends on their income, their tastes, and the price of substitute staples such as corn. In general, the demand for food is quite unresponsive to price changes because there are no close substitutes. However, as we go to more clearly defined categories of food, the demand becomes much more responsive to price changes because of available substitutes. Even so, it does take quite a drastic reduction in the price of wheat to get people to buy a lot more. Conversely, an increase in price will not cause people to buy very much less. This has serious implications for farmers.

Farmers' production costs and output can and often do vary greatly from year to year due to, among other things, variations in weather. During a year when the climate is favourable output may be relatively large and the equilibrium price will necessarily have to be relatively low in order to induce consumers to buy the entire quantity supplied in this competitive, unregulated market situation.

The opposite will occur when production is relatively small in one year because of, for example, a drought. The price will rise greatly. Basically, then, the short run competitive market in wheat will see changing prices of the product and changing profits for the producers.

How does the above situation compare to the one that now prevails in the EEC? The difference is that farmers can sell their crops at prices supported by EEC countries. In other words, EEC countries make an open-ended commitment to buy whatever their farmers grow at a pre-ordained price, and this price obviously is above one that would prevail in the absence of the support system. Farmers, however, are not stupid, no matter which country they reside in. At higher prices, they produce more. In the United

States during the heyday of its price support system, farmers produced so much that the Government ended-up with thousands upon thousands of silos filled with millions upon millions of bushels of 'surplus' wheat, corn, etc. The way the Americans tried to solve the problem was by imposing production quotas and restricting the acreage that could be tilled. European countries, however, don't seem to have this anti-surplus mechanism. What has happened in the past is the stockpiling of over-priced food at home (do you remember the mountains of butter?) or the dumping of surpluses in non-EEC countries.

It is interesting to note that the European system of farm subsidization works exactly the same way the American one has. That is to say, the only people who can benefit from such a system are large farmers. Obviously, when the price of a particular product is supported, the farmers benefit in proportion to their production. Poor farmers are by definition poor because they produce very little. Rich farmers are by definition rich because they produce a lot. The EEC Common Agricultural Policy has benefited farmers in proportion to their production. Essentially, then, those who have gained very little have been French peasants, for example; those who have gained a lot have been the prosperous owners of rolling wheat farms in the Paris basin, as another example. It is not unusual to find the latter with incomes in the neighbourhood of £20,000. If, in fact, the CAP were really intended to help out the medium and small farmers in European countries, there would not be involved any type of price support system but rather it would give direct payment to farmers inversely proportional to their income.

It has been speculated that the only reason the EEC's farm policy has continued to work is because West Germany has been willing to subsidize France. In fact, one observer contends that

that has been the greatest success of the programme; the CAP has been a means by which West Germany could provide subsidies to France. Perhaps West Germany has been willing to pay agricultural subsidies to France by way of supporting agricultural prices in order to promote political unification of some sort. The facts speak for themselves. From 1958 to 1974, France has been estimated to have taken out of the European agricultural fund £600 million more than they put in. And, after all, the EEC gave French farmers a highly protected market and a system of guaranteed prices originally pegged to the highest levels prevailing in the members of the Six.

As can be expected, the consumer loses out in all of this by paying a higher price for his or her food products than would exist otherwise. It's strange that Communist-backed organizations in France have supported so strongly interference in the agricultural markets, for, presumably, communists are supposed to be supporting the Common Man. One such organization is called the *Mouvement de Defense de l'Exploitation Familiale.* This movement in early 1974 asked for State stockpiling of beef and a ban on exports. Why? Simply because imported meat had helped pull the beef prices down in France at that time and the stockpiling of beef by the Government would help support it at higher rates. So on both counts this *mouvement* would like to see beef prices higher. Obviously, this benefits beef farmers, and hurts consumers.

Some European governments do, however, worry about the price of food to the consumer. The remedies to high food prices are, however, often quite devious. For example, when Britain's Labour Government attempted to smooth out the effects of some bad inflationary shocks in the early spring of 1974, it rammed through a Budget which included about £500 million for new subsidies on bread, milk, and other basic foods. But governments cannot get resources out of thin air. Increased subsidies on basic foods to low-income groups in Britain would have to be paid for out of either increased taxes or reductions in other Government spending. So, in order to finance such subsidization, the British Government then decided to impose increased taxes on tobacco, liquor, and similar items. What did this mean? Low-income groups were to have cheap food but relatively more expensive luxuries. It's not obvious that such a programme would in fact leave low-income consumers any better off.

At this point, one might ask why food products should occupy such a special category in governmental thinking about prices, production, and profits. It is not true that there must be a price support system in order to keep farmers producing food that you and I can eat. Agriculture is just like any other business. If the relative rate of return goes up, more capital will flow into it and there will be more production. If the relative rate of return falls, capital will flow out of it with the opposite result. Prices for food products without Government intervention will not become prohibitive so that no one can afford to eat. They never did in the recent past, so why should they in the future? The arguments for subsidizing food, or subsidizing farmers, really rest on value judgments. If, for example, you believe that the gain to farmers at a cost to consumers is appropriate, then you would support the EEC's Common Agricultural Policy. If you believe that the cost to subsidizing food should be paid for by taxing luxuries, then you might agree with a recent British policy. In both instances, however, there may be more efficient means of obtaining the social goals you wish.

Chapter 9

The Economics of Speculating in Whiskey

A few years ago, a report from the Warden Walker Worldwide Investment Company indicated that if you invested in raw Scotch, you could double your money in four years. The reasoning went as follows. After whiskey is distilled, it is stored in bonded warehouses for three or four years while it matures. The idea is for the private investor to buy the whiskey cheaply from the distillery, then sell it for a handsome capital gain later, after it has matured.

And to prove its point, Warden Walker claimed that investors who did this every year for the past twenty-four years would have averaged an annual profit of 34 per cent. Is it true that an investment in Scotch whiskey is going to yield you a higher than normal rate of return? The fact of the matter is you have as good a chance of making a high rate of return investing in whiskey as you do investing in any other similar type of investment that carries the same amount of risk. This is a shocking assertion, and one that most investors will never admit. It's especially true for those individuals who play the Stock Market. They are convinced that with enough investigation of potential 'winners', they can make a lot of money. Or, alternatively, they are convinced that if they study the past behaviour of stock prices enough, they can discern definite patterns and cash-in on the next upswing. Or, as something else to try, they might be convinced that if they find a hot stockbroker, he can tell them which stocks are going to increase in price, or what the market will do in general.

Before you decide whether the information about Scotch whiskey is relevant to your investment decision, or whether the information that your local stockbroker gives you is accurate, you should consider some of the implications of the fact that the Stock Market in every country in the world is the most perfectly competitive market we know. The Scotch market may not be as perfectly competitive, but it is still one in which information flows quite freely. When we talk about such a market, we mean that there are a large number of buyers and sellers, the product is uniform, and no buyer or seller can usually influence the market. There are two implications of this competitive market which must be kept in mind.

First, information is cheap and abundant. This is another way of saying that what you know everyone else knows, too. Second, every time you buy a stock, someone else is selling that stock. Or, to put it another way, every time you are betting that the stock is going to go up, someone else is betting that it is going down. That is not quite accurate; a more precise statement is that your purchase reflects your judgment that, given your information about all the alternative ways you could invest your money, Stock X is the most likely to yield you the highest return. The seller of Stock X is making the judgment that some alternative use of his funds will yield him a higher return. Is your information better than his? Not unless you have some inside source unknown to others.

For example, suppose you read in tomorrow's *Economist* that the management of Volvo has just announced a new breakthrough in engine design. The discovery will allow Volvo to make cars cheaper than Saab, Fiat, Bavarian Motor Works, and Rolls Royce. Should you immediately phone your broker and place a buy order for some Volvo shares? Go ahead if you want to, but do not expect to make a fortune. Remember, the market is competitive. The information in the *Economist* would already be completely capitalized on by the time you see it. That means public information will not help you on your road to financial success. By the time you get the news about Volvo, or any other company for that matter, there will have been enough buyers who 'got there first' so that the price of the stock will reflect the new profits picture.

At any moment in time, the price of any stock reflects all existing information on the profit outlook of each listed company. What is more, the average investor does not need to know what is happening for this last statement to be true. Only a few investors need be informed because they and their friends will want to take advantage of all new pieces of relevant information.

The way they take advantage of any new information is by buying or selling. The price of the stock goes up or down until all new information is fully discounted - i.e. capitalized to the present.

We can just as easily apply the above reasoning to information contained in any investors' newsletter. Most large brokerage firms have research departments where numerous stock analysts check up on good and bad buys. If you do business with one of these firms, you can probably get research information on hundreds, if not thousands, of companies. But so can anybody else. Since it does not take everyone acting in the market to get the price of a stock moving up or down, how useful can such research information be? True, you will know more about each company you read about, but what you are after as an investor is a return on your money and time invested. Since information flows so quickly, what you read about in some brokerage house's newsletter is not going to give you the advantage over the next person. We repeat: by the time you see information printed somewhere, it is of no use to you; it has already been capitalized upon.

Now, let us look at the man who should know what to tell you - your stockbroker. No doubt he is willing to suggest numerous good buys. He might even have some special schemes if you are one of his preferred customers. Again, we apply the competitive nature of the market in an analysis of your broker's hot tips. Unless he has inside information that no one else has heard about, what he tells you is as good as what you might decide for yourself.

Since the chances of his giving away really valuable inside information are close to zero, we must conclude that the value of his choice words must be in other than helping you get a higher than average rate of return on your money invested.

To prove my point, we can look at the experiences in both Europe and the United States. Let's look, for a moment, at the average yield in the American Stock Market and compare it with the result which we would get by randomly selecting, say, eight stocks. The average yield of stocks on the New York Stock Exchange, left in for varied periods of time, averages about a 10 to 12 per cent rate of return where dividends are all re-invested. By random, we mean a selection of stocks picked by throwing a dart at the stock page, or by using a table of random numbers to tell you which one to choose. If you picked eight stocks in that manner, the chances would have been 95 out of 100 that you would have realized this average return.

A careful study of thirty countries including those in Europe and the Orient indicated that a comprehensive group of stock will protect against inflation apart from hyper-inflation or wartime devastation. Stocks, compared with bonds or other fixed value assets, if broadly selected, pass the test as an inflation hedge for long-term holdings. As an example, during the twenty-year period after 1950, the value of stocks corrected for price changes rose 247 per cent in Austria, 207 per cent in Finland, 169 per cent in France, 718 per cent in Germany, 146 per cent in Italy, 125 per cent in Sweden, 110 per cent in Switzerland, and 98 per cent in the United Kingdom.

I am not suggesting that every investor should randomly select eight stocks in which he periodically puts his cash, for that will yield only the average rate of return. Some people want more than the average; in fact, all do. But the price of getting higher than average returns is a higher risk. You as an investor can invest in very speculative new issues, mining stocks, and the like. You will then have a very small chance of getting a relatively high return, and also a very large chance of getting a relatively low return (even negative). Nothing is obtained without a cost. If you strike it rich, it will be due mostly to luck and certainly not to your special feel for the market. Once you realize this, you will be able to apply the above analysis to all types of investments and schemes. I leave it to you to decide what your reaction should be to the first paragraph of this chapter.

Chapter 10

The Economics of Telephone and Mail Service

In most of the world today, mail service is a government monopoly. In not all of the world today, however, is telephone communication a nationalized industry. Before we go into some analysis of why so many people in West Germany, France, the United Kingdom and elsewhere are quite dissatisfied with the relatively high postage rates they must pay coupled with relatively poor service, we will first look into a comparison between the European nationalized telephone system and the one that prevails in the United States.

Today the United States leads the world with sixty telephones per hundred population. The numbers for the EEC are quite different: Britain, 29 per 100; Germany, 25; Italy, 19; and France, only 18.5. Now, part of this difference can, of course, be attributed to the larger *per capita* incomes or standard of living that are experienced by North Americans as opposed to Europeans. And, of course, another part can be explained by the Americans' mania for gadgets. But only a part. France's *per capita* income is certainly not only 30 per cent of the United States'. A more fruitful line of analysis might be conducted by examining the different incentive systems that are used in the two different systems.

In the United States, telephone companies, although regulated by the Government, are privately owned. When a new innovation is discovered and put into service, the resulting extra profits can be garnered by the stockholders in the privately-owned telephone companies. Who receives what when a similar innovation is possible in the French, British, Scandinavian, or West German systems? Obviously not the stockholders because there are none; the Government owns and operates these systems. Consequently, the incentive for the managers of European nationalized telephone systems are quite different than for the managers and stockholders in the American system. It is not surprising that the rate of innovation in European telephone systems is quite a bit less than the rate of innovation in the American one.

It is also true that the government-operated British and European telephone systems have until recently been locked into a rigid 'buy national' equipment purchasing tradition, thus steadily lagging behind United States service standards. Recently, however, pressed both by public demand and massive changes in technology, a telephone boom of unprecedented proportions is opening up in the Common Market countries.

Besides the expensive 'buy national' policies that have been followed by British, French, and other nationalized systems, these systems have generally been unresponsive to excessive demands on their systems. And one of the reasons they have been unresponsive is because they have not decided to charge individual telephone users the full social cost of the services acquired. As in all of the previous chapters' discussion, whenever the price of a good or service is held below a price that will equate supply with demand, there will be shortages, waiting lists, and dissatisfaction. This is the most obvious, and certainly the most correct, way to explain why, for example, in 1972, there were over one million West Germans on a waiting list for new telephone connections. Compare this to the situation in the United States where anyone in just about any place can obtain a new telephone within several days.

In an unrestricted situation in Europe and Britain where the telephone companies were run by individuals seeking to make the most profit possible, there would be no waiting lists and a greatly expanded phone system. And, in fact, prices might in the long run ultimately be lower, as they are in the United States relative to the rest of the world. How could this be?, you might ask. After all, wouldn't the profit-maximizing private individuals attempt to extract more money from telephone consumers than the government-run companies do today? Yes, they would, but in so doing, the following would occur. Say, for example, that today all of the EEC's telephone systems were handed over to individuals. Immediately you would find (assuming no regulation) that prices on telephone services would rise dramatically. This would decrease the quantity of telephone service demanded so that there would be no waiting lists, but at the same time, it would increase tremendously the profits made by the private owners of these telephone systems. There would be an incentive to modernize the systems much faster than they are being modernized now, and to look for cost-saving techniques that could be used to increase profits even more. As technology improved and the cost of providing services fell, the profit-maximizing owners of the telephone systems would find that to make even more profits, they could lower prices to induce more consumers to buy more telephone services. And, as an aside, the quality of telephone services would undoubtedly improve. (Of course, that is not saying much when one looks at the quality of service that exists, for example, in France where the centralized switching systems date back to the turn of the century.)

Now, the above argument is not to be construed as a plea for denationalization of the telephone service. Rather, it is an indication that the Government officials running the telephone service would make citizens better off if a price were charged for that service that equated supply and demand and any excess revenues were used to modernize the system so that later on prices could come down as the cost of providing services fell and the capacity to provide them increased.

The postal service is in a similar situation on the Continent, the British Isles, America, and just about everywhere else. The price charged for postal service is generally below the cost of providing it. The result is that the central governments of most countries in the world today must subsidize the national post offices. Losses on the postal service in Britain, for example, are probably in the neighbourhood of £70 million to £100 million a year, although this figure varies from year to year. In most countries of the world today, the losses are generally sustained on other than first-class mail. That is to say, users of first-class mail tend to subsidize, in addition to the government subsidy paid for by all taxpayers, users of second-, third-, and fourth-class mail. The latter are composed generally of advertisers and magazines and periodicals. The question that should be asked is: Does the public want to subsidize such activities? And, if so, could not the subsidy be in a direct form so that the public would know exactly how much it is paying for the luxury of having magazines sent to subscribers at prices which do not cover the full cost of mailing them?

As with the telephone services, the nationalized postal services have lagged behind in all countries of the world in improving its technology. Complaints about postal services increase every year, and nowhere are they more vociferous than in the United States. It is interesting to contrast the two situations, for in the United States one would expect that the technology is certainly available, as is the income to pay for it. Why is it that the telephone system is the most modern in the entire world, and for which there are relatively few complaints (except in some large cities), but the postal service is universally detested as an inefficient, bungling, backward affair? The difference, of course, is obvious. The telephone system is privately owned but regulated, whereas the post office system is owned by the Government. In the latter case, the incentives to the managers of the system are quite a bit different than in the former case. Post office managers cannot appropriate the gains from increased efficiency that they provide by improving the technology and the service. That is to say, they cannot expect to have increases in the value of any stocks in the company they hold, or to be offered higher salaries by the stockholders for managing the company in a way that generates higher profits.

The above argument, to repeat what was mentioned before, does not constitute a case for the de-nationalization of the postal service. It does, however, cause one to have serious thoughts about having government bureaucrats run the postal service, as well as the telephone service, in such a way that distorts the use of resources in the economy. If, in fact, subsidization of certain elements of the sectors of the economy is desired, a more direct means could be used and the public would know exactly how much it is paying for that subsidy. The way in which the post office is run does not allow such a situation to exist.

Chapter 11

The Economics of Usury Laws

There have always been restrictions on interest rates, both for the lender and for the borrower. Everybody seems to know that money-lenders have some unique monopolistic power over others in the economy. Indeed, money men have been attacked so much that dominant ethnic groups have historically shunned the profession, leaving it to minority groups. In the Western world, the Church had lots of rules against market exchanges used to obtain 'excessive' personal gain. For example, there were rules against usury - lending out money at interest, even very low interest. Today it is hard for us to imagine such a rule. Perhaps exorbitant interest rates are out of the question, but a zero rate? Why would anybody continuously be willing to give up the use of his own money for a certain period of time if he is not paid for it? Voluntary exchange must be mutually beneficial. Perhaps some people would be willing to give up the use of their money for a while because of love or philanthropy, but most didn't then and still don't. Strictures on interest rates are no different from strictures on a positive price being charged for any good or service.

During medieval times, the Church attempted to instill in the populace the notion that life on this earth was only temporary, ephemeral, and one should look to the hereafter. Thus, there was extreme disapproval of wealth lending, and in such a situation one could be expected not to care whether one got interest on money loaned out.

The concept of interest for money dates back to Roman times when, by law, the defaulting party to a contract had to pay his creditor a compensation. Medieval lawyers used the legal tactic of *damna et interesse* to extract such compensation. Thus, *interesse* became a charge for the use of money under the guise of indemnity for failure to perform a contract.

Apparently, modern man's enlightenment on the topic of interest rates has not completely changed the picture. We see throughout the world the persistence of legislation affecting the lending of money. There is obviously still a widespread suspicion that money-lenders are monopolistic, shady influences. Most countries set maximum interest rates on loans to consumers. To find out the consequences, let's examine the so-called money market.

The money market is like any other market. The people who supply money are individuals like you and me, and institutions, who merely obtain other individuals' money. We are willing at a price, called the interest rate, to forego the present command over goods and services to use today in order to have goods and services to use tomorrow. The higher the price we are offered for the use of our money, the more we will be willing to lend. The opposite occurs on the demand side. For those of us who want to borrow somebody else's money, we will demand a smaller quantity the higher the price. Who are those who create the demand? Consumers wanting to buy goods and services now and pay later, businessmen wanting to invest in new plant and equipment and governments.

The money market, of course, is not one single institution, like the Stock Market. But rather, it consists of multitudinous sub-markets, each for a particular purpose. There is a money market for property loans, commercial credit, consumer loans, etc. And generally, each sub-market will have its own institution to take care of lining up borrowers with lenders. Moreover, each sub-market generally has a different market clearing price in the absence of regulation. The effective rate of interest paid to borrow on a car is generally higher, for example, than the effective rate of interest paid to borrow on a house. A government can usually borrow money at a lower rate of interest than an individual or a private firm. All of these rates, of course fluctuate over time as they respond to changes in the supply and in the demand for loans.

How can we explain, though, the large differences there are in interest rates at any given moment? We can explain them by looking at the several factors which determine how much a loan costs an individual borrower. And the first of these determinants is the length of the loan: the longer the time period involved, the less certain the lender can be about what money market conditions will be at the time he is repaid. He therefore will ask for a higher compensation in the form of a higher interest rate. The next determinant of the price of loans is the degree of risk involved to the lender. The higher the risk, the higher the rate of interest that will be charged. And, lastly, the cost of administering the loan must be considered. There are certain fixed set-up expenses for any loan, no matter what its size. Therefore, this handling charge expressed as a percentage of the size of the loan is usually larger for smaller loans than for larger ones.

Suppliers of loans are going to respond to changing market conditions, just like suppliers of any other resource. They can be expected to shift their funds from one sub-market in the total money market to another, depending on where they can get the highest relative rate of return. That return is adjusted for time risk and handling charges. In order, of course, for them to know more about profitable opportunities for their loanable funds,they must have information. We know that in every country in the world today (just about) there are a wide variety of agencies and news media that dispense this type of information at a very low cost. Consequently, the overall money capital market tends to be extremely responsive to quite small changes in rates of return to relative suppliers of loanable funds.

Returning now to the question of usury laws, suppose that a government legislates that a maximum interest rate of 8 per cent can be charged for consumer loans. Obviously, if this interest rate, 8 per cent, is higher than the one prevailing in the market at that time, there will be no effect of the government legislation. However, in the event that the interest rate prevailing in the economy is higher - say, 12 or 15 or 20 per cent - there will be an effect. The restriction on interest rates will cause buyers to demand more loanable funds than suppliers are willing to supply given that return. What will happen is that lenders will begin to introduce service charges to cover handling costs which were formerly incorporated into the interest rate. They will also have to move to some sort of rationing of available funds for loans. What they would most logically and, in fact, do is attempt to eliminate the riskier loans. The riskiness of borrowers tends to be inversely related to the borrower's income. Consequently, an interest rate restriction in consumer loans will adversely affect low-income groups of people, for they will be discriminated against in the money market, relatively more than if there were no restrictions on the interest rates that can be charged for consumer loans.

It is difficult to see how consumers can be helped by interest rate restrictions when such a result obtains. Nonetheless, usury laws are rampant in the world today. The reason that consumers believe they are a 'good' is because consumers mistakenly think they can get loans at a lower price. In fact, some of them do. Those are the lucky ones who obtain loanable funds at a price that is below the price that would equate supply with demand. They obviously benefit from usury law legislation. And who are these consumers? As we pointed out above, they will generally be higher-income borrowers. The poor will in effect get nothing at all, and, in fact, lose out because they will be forced to go to unregulated markets or loan sharks.

The public may in fact believe that the reason interest rates must be regulated is because the loan market is monopolistic. If that were indeed the case, which it is not because there are thousands upon thousands of alternative lending institutions, then the correct procedure, or at least the most efficient one, for eliminating the monopolistic restrictions on loans is to break up the monopoly by anti-trust legislation and prosecution.

Everyone who lives in a country where the rate on mortgages is set at a maximum by the government concerned can attest to the pernicious, long-run effects - and short run, too - of such legislation. What has happened in the mortgage market in all countries where rates are regulated is the following: sellers of mortgages - i.e. lending institutions - cannot charge the rate of interest that equates the supply with the demand. What has happened, then, is that lower-income borrowers are discriminated against by the tactic of requiring very large down payments on mortgages. What has also happened is that various and sundry techniques to skirt the legal maximum on the mortgage interest rate have been devised, such as prepayment of interest, higher closing costs on deals, etc. What is ironic is that at the same time that numerous applicants of mortgages cannot get the mortgages they want because of the interest rate restriction, the supply of mortgages actually falls, causing the situation to worsen. Why does the quantity supplied fall? Because suppliers of funds find alternative outlets for their loanable funds where they can make relatively higher rates of return.

The question is really: Is it better to have no usury laws and higher interest rates, or to have usury laws, lower interest rates, but a larger number of applicants who cannot obtain credit?

Chapter 12

The Economics of Air Fares

The summer of 1971 will go down in the history of commercial aviation as the beginning of the end. Some 'unscrupulous' foreign airline companies decided that they would break the international air travel cartel wide open by offering regularly scheduled cheap flights from Europe to North America. Waves of 'predatory' pricing of trans-Atlantic air travel have abounded since then. At the beginning of this decade, Pan American and other American airlines had been badly beaten by charter flights and unscheduled airlines flying across the Atlantic. In the United States, Icelandic Airlines was one of the first companies to offer scheduled cheap flights in order to undercut members of the worldwide cartel conspiracy, called the International Air Transport Association (IATA). However, in order for Icelandic to continue those flights, the only European country in which it could land was Luxembourg, which had not been a member of the organization.

Icelandic's success attracted numerous other pricecutters into the market and the charter flight boom began. Commercial airlines around the world finally gave up on the world wide price-fixing cartel and decided to cut trans-Atlantic fares in order to recapture their share of the growing international air travel market. Back in the spring of 1971 when Alitalia announced it was going to offer the lowest Europe-North America round trip yet, whether or not other members of the cartel agreed, the seams started splitting on the IATA flag.

Four years after this dispute about North Atlantic air fares had been going on behind IATA's closed doors, BOAC, in exasperation, resorted to a public showdown. BOAC started using its veto power to make sure that no new world wide air fare schedule could be agreed upon by the IATA members. Back in February of 1973, fares then fell out of IATA's hands, to be determined by governments between themselves.

In general, any cartel arrangement that is set up in order to restrict the output of a product or service and therefore keep the price up is doomed to failure. The reason is easy to see. The incentive to cheat on the cartel arrangement is great because if everyone abides by the high price/low output agreement, except one nation, company, or person (whatever the case may be), then that cheat will in fact gain relatively large amounts of business by cutting prices just a little bit. The history of cartels is one of dissolutions and failure. Witness how poorly the Organization of Petroleum Exporting Countries (OPEC) kept together during the so-called boycott of European and American oil in 1973 and 1974. The question remains, then, if cartels are inherently unstable and it is to the advantage of each individual member to cheat, how has IATA remained in existence for so long? The answer is not hard to find: members of IATA are supported by governmental protection. Governments either regulate airline companies in each country in the world, or actually own the companies themselves. Without governmental support of such cartel arrangements, IATA would have failed a long time ago.

Even during the years when it was considerably stronger than it is today, IATA was still faced with the problem of competition among the ranks. That competition at first did not present itself in an obvious manner. It was waged by changing the quality of the service offered to various international air travellers. Several companies, for example, competing on a North Atlantic route which could not offer lower fares, could, nonetheless, offer better food, larger lounges, better movies, and bigger drinks, and that's exactly what happened. They also could offer more numerous and more convenient flights. Herein lies one of the reasons that for a large part of the history of IATA, international air carriers flew at less than full capacity. Take the example of two airlines flying from London to New York. Neither one can offer a lower price because they are members of IATA. What they can do,

however, is offer more numerous flights. When will they stop
adding flights? When the additional cost of adding another plane
outweighs the additional revenues obtained by adding that plane.
Throughout the regulated world of airline travel, half-filled planes
are commonplace because of the inability of airlines to compete
on a price basis.

The incentive has always been there for alternative schemes to be
worked out by profit-seeking entrepreneurs who wanted to capture
some of the international air market. That is why we saw the
large increase in charter flights. Charter flights could be offered at
rates that were not governed by IATA conference. Increasingly,
charters had taken away more and more of regularly scheduled
airlines' North Atlantic travel.

Perhaps now after this discussion you can understand why, for
example, the service, food, and accommodations on air travel,
within, say, France are much worse than the service, food, and
accommodations on air travel internationally. Air France is owned
by the French Government, as is Air Inter. The latter flies only in
the interior of the country. There is no competition allowed; no
other company has the right to establish a domestic service in
France. However, Air France is in competition with numerous
other international air carriers on many of the major international
routes. Since it cannot compete on the basis of price, it offers
better service.

There is a question as to whether nationally-owned or regulated air
carriers should be rescued from 'cheap' foreign competition. Let's
say, for example, that complete unrestrained international
competition were alive and would drive out some of the larger
airline companies in the world. Are the people in those countries
that lose their airlines worse off? No. Only those who are
stockholders in the private bankrupt airlines and those whose

specialized skills which allow them a higher than market wage while working for the companies now bankrupt are worse off. Otherwise, the rest of the people would be better off. What they would do is substitute the new lower priced (foreign) air travel for higher priced air travel. If foreign competitors can offer nationals an air fare at a lower cost than the nationals' own company or companies can, then those citizens are better off (taken as a society) by flying in other countries' airlines. This argument is no different than the one which underlies competition within any country. If you make shoes, and so does your neighbour down the street, but he is more efficient than you and, consequently, drives you out of business, your bankruptcy will increase the overall efficiency in the use of resources available. You lose, but the rest of society gains. If you accept the fact that inefficient businesses should not be subsidized domestically when they're faced with more efficient domestic competition, then you should not be in favour of subsidizing domestic producers of air travel who cannot compete with more efficient foreign producers.

Chapter 13

The Economics of Consumerism

Caveat emptor - let the buyer beware. Until recently the public and government were content to allow Adam Smith's famous 'invisible hand' to maximize the welfare of the nation. Times have changed, though. The dictum, *caveat emptor*, no longer seems to be appropriate. The age of consumerism is upon us, heralded by the exposés of North America's Ralph Nader, Sweden's Bjorn Gillberg, and others. Consulted by presidents and politicians, and encouraged by continued support at the popular level, active control of business practices by government has become more and more of a reality in practically every country throughout the world. Businessmen can no longer assume that it is the buyer's responsibility to ensure that the businessman has made a safe product, produced a healthy food, or been fair in his advertising. The age of consumerism has brought with it a reversal of roles. The businessman must be the one to make sure that he sells a product which is safe for consumption. If he fails in his task, he can now be sued and even put in gaol in some countries.

Throughout many countries, including Britain, the United States, and Europe, there has been a growth in consumer protection agencies or local consumer advice centres. The one proposed by Sir Geoffrey Howe as part of a national network has been slow in getting off the ground, but may in fact turn into something really large. The private British Consumers' Association has also been attempting to finance consumer groups and advice centres.

What does standard economic theory have to say about the need for legislation to prevent businessmen from defrauding the public with unhealthy foods, unsafe products, and unsubstantial advertising claims? Economics tells us that the forces of market competition will obviate any need for regulation. Let us take an example. Suppose that, unknown to you, there is a fraudulent television repair man in your neighbourhood. When your set breaks down you call him in. He says that a lot more is wrong with it than actually is the case. You have no way of knowing whether he is telling the truth because you do not possess the technical knowledge that he has. If you believe him, you are defrauded. He charges you a higher price than you should be charged. Let us say he takes the set into his shop, replaces two or three valves that cost him about £2 total, and brings the set back to you. He then gives you a bill for £20, saying that three transformers had blown out and fourteen valves had to be replaced. You cry in anguish but pay the bill anyway. You have been defrauded.

It matters little in economic analysis whether the repair man tells you that he is going to replace two valves for £20, or whether he lies to you and says that your television needed three transformers and fourteen valves and, therefore, your charge is £20. You pay the same one way or the other. It matters little to you whether he lies or not - you still received a bill for £20.

If there is any competition you would expect high-priced (fraudulent) repair men to lose all their business. The competitive process, though, takes time. Information costs are not zero. It takes time for so-called honest repair men to make themselves known to prospective customers, and it takes time for a customer to find out about such honest repair men. Competition among repair men will, according to standard theory, eventually lead to elimination of dishonest repair men. After all, people will seek out the honest ones.

We know that competition will act faster in certain circumstances. In this particular case, if we are in a community which has a relatively stable or fixed citizenry we would expect that the dishonest repair men would be run out of business faster than if the community in question were unstable. In the former, neighbours would all know which repair men were dishonest.

In the latter, the dishonest repair men could go to the unsuspecting newcomers to get business. We would expect, therefore, that there are fewer dishonest repair men in small towns which have very little movement of population than in large cities.

Since manufacturers of television sets have a stake in the repair costs of their products, we would also expect that they would try to do something about reducing them. After all, you are actually purchasing the *services* of a television, not the television set. The services per unit time are a function both of the price you paid for the set and how much you have to pay for repairs to keep it running in good condition. The higher the price you have to pay for repairs, the higher the price per unit of service flow from that set. If maintenance mechanics have somehow conspired to keep the price per constant quality unit of service repairs artificially high, then we would expect television manufacturers to have an incentive to reduce the need for repairs in their machines. That would reduce the price for television services and increase the demand for televisions. In fact, we have found that some companies are manufacturing sets which are easily maintained; there is at least one television on the market now with little units that can be pulled out of the back and replaced cheaply.

Why, then, is it necessary today to have consumer protection so that people cannot be cheated by television repair men? In the first place, even if we assume that competition will eventually lead to the elimination of fraudulent television repair men, the adjustment time may be unacceptably long from a social stand-point. It may be socially cheaper for consumer protection agencies to spot-check television service men in order to weed out those who are lying to their customers about the extent of both necessary repairs and those that were actually performed.

In what circumstances would we expect that the adjustment time would be unacceptably long? If, for some reason, the population were becoming more and more unstable - i.e. the number of times people moved on the average in their lifetime was increasing - we would expect that information about dishonest repair men would not be as well known as in a situation where the population was more stable. If in fact the Scandinavians, the British and Europeans in general have increased their mobility, then this will lengthen the adjustment time necessary for competition among television repair men to weed out the most dishonest among them. If such is the case, then consumer protection may seem more necessary than in the past.

There are other reasons why information costs have become higher and, therefore, the adjustment times have become longer. Presumably, as products become more complex it is more difficult for consumers to understand what they are buying. Therefore, they are easier prey for unscrupulous repair men because they cannot understand anything that is told them. This may have been the case for a while with television sets. (As we said before, though, the trend is toward less complicated machines that can be serviced merely by replacing small units that are easily accessible.)

Let us turn now from protection against fraudulent servicing practices to the concern about the ingredients in food products. For a number of years there has been concern by consumer protection agents. Suppose that government officials are concerned about the fat content in bratwurst. Or, consumerists are concerned about the amount of ingredients in bratwurst that haven't traditionally been included. Again, we can apply our standard microeconomic model to find out what it has to say about the fat content of bratwurst.

Remember that when we talked about fraudulent television repair practices, we said that we could actually translate them into a higher price per constant quality unit of service being charged. The same thing is true for bratwurst. The price of bratwurst should not be viewed in our analysis as merely the price of bratwurst, but rather the price of a unit of bratwurst of constant quality. If the price of bratwurst remains the same and the fat content increases, then the price per constant quality unit has gone up, assuming, of course, that the actual meat content of bratwurst is important to the consumer. If, for example, only the taste of the bratwurst is important and not its food value, then quality will have to be measured in terms of taste and not, say, in calories or vitamins. If an increase in the fat content of bratwurst does not lead to a deterioration in the taste, then the price has not changed.

Let us take an individual firm and assume for the moment that consumers are unable to assess the food value of bratwurst. Also, assume that the fat content of bratwurst does not alter its taste. In such a case, why would not an individual, profit-maximizing producer make bratwurst that had 99.99 per cent fat? The only thing that was not fat would be the skin. After all, fat is cheaper than real meat. Would not this profit-maximizing firm be able to make more profits if it could charge the same price and lower the cost of production? Yes, it would. Why is there not more fat than we currently find if such is the case? The reasons, obviously, are:

1   Fat content does alter the taste of the bratwurst.

2   Consumers can, at least on the margin, discover how much food value there is in a bratwurst and are interested in that statistic.

3   There is competition among bratwurst producers so that one of them cannot get away with fooling the public for very long.

Consumer protection in the form of refusing bratwurst manufacturers the right to increase the fat content of their product can, nonetheless, serve the purpose of increasing information in the market place and decreasing uncertainty. If everybody knows that the maximum amount of fat allowed in bratwurst is, say, 20 per cent, then nobody need worry about the possibility of getting a 90 per cent fat bratwurst. The search costs to the buying public are, therefore, reduced. One might wish, though, not only to assess the benefits but also the costs of such consumer protection. Moreover, one might want to distinguish between what he thinks people should be buying and what people themselves actually want to buy. Such questions are in the realm of normative economics.

An alternative policy might involve forcing accurate labelling of the contents of food products. Each consumer could then buy exactly what he wanted and would know exactly what he was buying. In other words, government regulation could seek to improve information about products instead of restricting their various characteristics to some governmentally 'acceptable' norm.

Chapter 14

The Economics of the Media

The production of radio and television signals is either wholly or at least in part a state monopoly in Britain and throughout most of Europe. In contrast, the production and dissemination of radio and television signals in the United States, although regulated by the Government, is a private affair. In all countries, the information that is disseminated by radio and television occupies a central part in the total information picture because of the pervasiveness of radio and television ownership and the time spent in viewing and listening to these forms of media by the public. In this short chapter, we will attempt to answer the following question: Does it matter who owns these forms of information dissemination? To answer this question we look at only two polar extremes. In one case, the government has complete ownership of radio and television signals; in the other extreme, there is unconstrained competition.

CASE 1: private ownership of property rights in radio and television signals. To establish the reasonableness of this polar case, we must make some assumptions about the mechanism by which property rights in the signals are enforced. It is possible, for example, for one signal to jam another and therefore cause economic damage. We will assume for the purposes of this discussion that the Courts will enforce property rights in well-defined geographic areas. We can assume, for example, that the entire electromagnetic spectrum is put up for auction to the highest bidder. Once the bidding is over, the Courts at nominal costs enforce the well-defined property rights. Hence, we have no technological problems about overcrowding.

Now we ask ourselves what type of information will be produced and disseminated if the entire electromagnetic spectrum is in private hands. First, since the spectrum is so large, we can assume that competition will prevail. It would generally not be profitable for a single private concern to purchase the entire spectrum.

There is a problem here concerning the public goods nature of the product under study. However, in countries where private ownership, although limited to less than the technologically complete number of stations, is allowed, that problem is usually solved in any of three ways:

1 the consumers of radio or television signals support the programmes by buying more of the goods and services advertised on those programmes;

2 listener subscription-type arrangements (which sometimes work, although with difficulty); and

3 through the use of a scrambler/de-scrambler system, pay-television and/or pay-radio can be utilised.

Now, under the above assumptions, the behaviour of the owners of property rights in the various stations can be analysed in exactly the same manner in which one analyses the behaviour of any other producer. In this particular case, the producer happens to produce information along with entertainment. Information and entertainment may at times coincide and, in fact, it is often difficult to separate the two because of the subjective nature of the definitions.

Since we can without much argument assume that in any given country or location, tastes will be different for many individuals, there will be numerous potential types of information and entertainment packages that can be sold through electromagnetic signals. In an attempt to maximize profits, owners of transmission bodies will compete with each other to furnish the most profitable packages. But just as one finds numerous types and qualities of motor-cars, shoes, and dresses, one would expect to find competition among owners of radio and television signals to cause them to devise numerous types of information and entertainment packages to sell listeners and viewers. It would be expected, then, that certain stations would emit lengthy political broadcasts, others not; certain stations would broadcast, along with classical music, commentaries on the cinema and poetry, whereas others would not, and so on.

The incentives for those running each individual station will be such in this situation that the public will receive information and entertainment which maximizes wealth from the resources used. This result is no different than the same result that obtains in a competitive system using scarce resources to produce any other product. If, for example, a station that is operated under a pay system with a scrambler/de-scrambler does not notice a change in taste for the information it is supplying, the consequences of that oversight would be immediately felt as revenues will fall. The incentive here for the managers of that station are obvious. Market surveys can be taken and a more appealing information/ entertainment package can be worked up in order to bring revenues back to more profitable levels. The bureaucracy within each privately-owned station will be constrained in its behaviour or by the yearly net profits of the station.

The information/entertainment package that is provided by any privately-owned station may, of course, be made up to reflect merely the tastes of the station's owner. However, if his tastes do not coincide with those of the market place, he (or the stockholders if the station is incorporated) in fact will have to pay for the production and dissemination in the form of a reduced net wealth position. Obviously, then, even a perfectly competitive system, as discussed here, does not prevent the production and dissemination of biased information or information that the market place deems false. However, as we shall see below in Case 2, under a competitive system the costs of biased information dissemination are higher both to the producer of it and to the recipients.

CASE 2: complete government control of radio and television signals. In this case, no private ownership of electromagnetic signal dissemination systems is allowed. The government is the sole owner of all radio and television stations, and, furthermore, decides the number of those stations that will remain extant, and the technical quality of the signals which are transmitted. Under this system, the incentives are different than in the previous one for those running the stations. In the government-controlled situation, the desire is to maximize the audience size so as to disseminate information to the largest number of people. The government-owned and -operated radio and television stations may in fact have a larger potential audience than in Case 1 above because the government may decide to build larger and more powerful transmitting systems to reach a larger audience. The 'revenue' obtained from reaching additional citizens is of course not measured in monetary terms, as it is in Case 1. However, it can be measured in some other terms such as political stability, etc. What is important to note here is that in this system, payment for radio and television information/entertainment packages is done through taxes. It is the political process, rather than the market process, which determines the size of the budget for information production and transmission by radio and television. This may lead to an over-production of radio and television signals, or to an under-production. If one judges casual empirical evidence today across countries, the latter seems to be a more distinct possibility.

It is probable that one sees such a dearth of radio and television stations in nations where the government owns and operates them because of the increasing costs of monitoring on the part of the government. That is to say, if the government has a particular set of information that it wants produced and disseminated about the country itself and the rest of the world, the smaller the number of radio and television stations that it runs, the smaller the monitoring job on the bureaucrats who run those stations. It would certainly be more costly to monitor the large number of radio stations that exist in the United States than it would be to monitor the small number that exist in France, for example, if the Government owned them in both cases. Obviously there are marginal benefits to increasing the number of stations in the government-owned situation, and these must be compared to the marginal costs of monitoring. Apparently, the latter exceed the former after a very small number.

Let us ask ourselves how the civil rather than private bureaucrat running the radio or television station will act. He will act, as in all cases, to maximize his own wealth position. In this particular instance, part of his wealth is psychic. He can receive psychic income from choosing particular programmes to be shown or heard on television and radio. In Case 1 above, the person deciding on the content of the programme could still obtain psychic income from choosing programmes that pleased him, but if his taste did not correspond to those of the market, profits would fall. In Case 2 here, by definition the product of programmes is a monopolist. He has no competition and can therefore obtain a higher amount of psychic income from catering to his own tastes than in the situation previously discussed where there is purely private ownership of stations.

The key to understanding the political economy of radio and television broadcasting lies in the monopolistic nature of the situation when the government has complete property rights in the electromagnetic spectrum. We pointed out above that any broadcaster, even in a perfectly competitive situation, can distort information, can suppress ideas, and can do anything he or she wishes in an effort to convert people in his or her market to his or her personal views. However, if the broadcaster is a monopolist - i.e. a government - the cost of information suppression and distortion is certainly less than in a competitive market. And that is for two reasons:

1   the control of information by the monopolist often prevents the listener or viewer from realizing that it is being misinformed, or that any other information actually exists, and

2   the listening or viewing audience has no substitutes to which it can turn - i.e. the demand curve facing the monopolist broadcaster is certainly much more in-elastic than the demand curve facing the competitive broadcaster.

It is interesting to note that the costs of distorting and suppressing information are greater to the audience in a monopoly broadcasting situation than to the audience facing competition among broadcasters. In the latter case, it matters little if one broadcaster distorts and suppresses information because that distortion and suppression do not deprive the listener or viewer of access to a presumably large alternative range of competing information/entertainment packages. Essentially, then, a monopolistic broadcaster will and can suppress the demand for competing products in the information field.

Of course, broadcasting is itself merely an intermediary product between the production and the consumption of information. A monopolist will attempt to present those ideas that consumers want most if he is maximizing total revenues; to do otherwise would be expensive. However, in the case where the government owns all of the means of information dissemination by radio and television, the revenues are not measured in monetary terms, as mentioned above. Rather, they may be measured in, for example, the quantity of propaganda absorbed by the population.

It is interesting to examine in some detail the results of more or

less free competition in television. This essentially has occurred in
Canada. Because of the proliferation of cables which allow the
transmission of a large number of television channels to
subscribing viewers, the possibility for having multitudinous
television stations in any one area has increased greatly. In Canada
the Government has allowed the proliferation of cable-diffused
television channels. For example, in the Province of Quebec there
are about 110 cable-diffusion enterprises, each one serving from
100 to 100,000 subscribers, or more than 20 per cent of the
homes in that area. In Montreal, for example, viewers have their
choice between eleven channels. The costs involved are trivial
compared to normal network expenses, or those incurred by
governments running their own national television stations. A
transmitter costs around 5,000 Canadian dollars, or less than
25,000 French francs. On a budget of around $20,000 to $25,000,
a television station can be started. This is the price that, for
example, the French Government-owned television system pays
for one colour video camera. Actually, it is only in the recent past
that such inexpensive equipment was sufficiently improved to
allow it to be used to help transmit a picture of a quality similar
to more expensive systems.

Television stations in Canada are run by everybody from high-
school students to retired taxi drivers. It is obvious also that the
types of programmes these neophytes produce please the Canadian
audiences. In one small town, for example, Gatineau, Ontario,
during the hours of 6.00pm to 7.30pm and on Sunday from
9.30am on, the local Channel 2 has a viewing audience in excess
of 50 per cent, in spite of the competition with the national
channel.

Some of the possible uses of such a large number of media outlets
which have easy access to an audience would, of course, be
anathema to governments desirous of limiting discussion on

sensitive issues. In Canada, the television is even used for local protests against rules and regulations deemed unacceptable to those hurt by them. In one town, high-school students protested on the local cable television channel against the regulation that they could not have long hair. The next day school officials were allowed to air their views on the same channel. A few days later, the rule was changed.

Interestingly, when European journalists living in countries with total government control over radio and television comment on the Canadian experience, there is rarely any mention of the possibility of duplicating that experience in Europe.*

*See, for example, *L'Express*, 23-29 July 1973, pp. 34-37

Chapter 15

The Economics of Flood Control

In the Netherlands, there is a constant battle against the sea. And even today, the delta region may still be considered a danger zone. For here the many outlets of the rivers Rhine and Maas drain into the North Sea. There are counter-attacking high tides which push into the maze of estuaries contaminating the soil, and occasionally storms reek devastation on the land.

To counter such problems with the ocean on its shores, the Dutch Government in 1954 launched a £500,000,000 Delta Project. According to the plan, fortifications would be built up and completed by 1978, keeping out the ocean from the Delta region forever.

The four massive dams shortened the coast line by about 600 kilometres. The three southerly barriers transformed tidal estuaries into an island-dotted freshwater lake, the Zeeuwse Meer. Inland, the Volkerak Dam separated the Zeeuwse Meer from the main outlet of the Rhine and Maas - the Haringvliet. The coastal Haringvliet Dam closes this outlet. The river water, seeking other access to the sea, escapes near Dordrecht into channels that flow through Rotterdam harbour. The seaward surge checks the tides' inland push, and flushes brine from the soil. The highways atop the new dams and the isolation of delta islands and peninsulas open the area as a recreational bonanza.

This final answer to flooding in the Netherlands is a system of massive barrier dams. The idea is to let the fresh water out while countering the tidal surges that put pressure on the dikes.

How are these dams financed? After all, the Dutch Government cannot obtain resources out of the sky. These dams are financed like any other government investment - i.e. by taxation on all the residents of Holland. Normally, flood control is a local tax matter with those directly affected paying for maintaining the dikes. But because of a system of tax credits for forming the new land below sea level, the tax burden for flood control has effectively been shifted to those who live on land above sea level. This is quite a nice trick: flood control in Holland allows owners of new land to get the benefits while those who live on the land above the previous sea-level end up paying the costs.

An alternative to flood control via expensive dams can be found in a fairly recent American system whereby the national Government insures owners of property in flood-prone areas for any flood losses that occur. Approximately 10,000 cities and towns along that nation's ocean, lake, and river fronts have been designated 'flood-prone'. This is not actually much different to the Dutch system in the sense that people who live in no-flood-prone areas end up subsidizing people who live in flood-prone areas, for the general tax fund is the source of monies that go to pay for those areas damaged by floods.

An interesting offshoot of the American system is the way in which the national Government has used its new flood insurance programme to dictate where and how buildings can be put up in the designated flood-prone areas. The American Federal Insurance Administration has issued extremely stringent ordinance and building codes that property-owners must comply with in order to obtain Governmental flood insurance. What the Government is obviously doing is attempting to reduce the future costs of flood damage and, thus, of the insurance programme. The national Government is therefore forcing local authorities to exercise more control over what is built in the affected areas. The regulations have been set forth such that they are virtually mandatory. What has happened, then, is that the national Government is telling people in many areas that they cannot build in flood-prone districts or that, if they want to, the construction must be exceedingly costly. If a community does not enact such a regulation, prospective owners cannot buy federal blood insurance and without that insurance, no Government-regulated bank or home loan company will be permitted to make a construction loan or grant a home mortgage.

In both the American case and the Dutch case, some people are benefiting while others are paying the costs for those benefits. In the Dutch case, the Government instituted direct construction activities whereas in the American case, the Government, in a more roundabout method, has dictated the particular types of construction activities that can be undertaken in flood-prone cases. In both cases, the governments have exercised a control that leads to an allocation of resources that probably differs substantially from what would have occurred in the absence of the legislation. Whether or not you believe such government activity to be 'correct' is, of course, a subjective matter. The fact that those who benefit from such government activity are not the ones who pay is again another matter for your subjective evaluation.

Chapter 16

The Economics of Welfare

'Cradle to grave' welfare assistance is almost a reality in a number of countries, including Britain, Denmark and Sweden. Recently, however, there has been a sort of anti-welfare revolution going on. We will see that reasons are not hard to find for such a reaction to the extension of government assistance to private individuals.

For years Scandinavia has been the model of democratic socialism with welfare systems that assure everybody of life's essentials. Not surprisingly, though, the price has been enormous bureaucracy, staggering tax rates, and an inevitable loss of individual initiative. For some Scandinavians, the Socialist dream has turned into a nightmare. Swedes decided to change things, and after 41 years, threw out their Socialist government. The long-standing Socialist majority in Norway diminished appreciably. Danes have expressed their discontent with the politicians running the country by voting for a party that literally hoped (and still does) to dismantle the Government. The party is headed by Mogens Glistrup, who, with the Progress Party, wants to get rid of large numbers of Denmark's 600,000 civil servants. Glistrup also wants to abolish all income taxes for those who make around 4,000 krone or less. 'Only fools pay income tax', Glistrup once said. 'There is no bigger crime against society than paying income tax.'

The Danes have a lot to complain about, for they are the most heavily-taxed of all industrialized people - fully 44 per cent of gross national product (GNP) is taken away in tax revenues. This can be compared with 40 per cent in Sweden, around 35 per cent in Britain, France and Germany, 28 per cent in Italy, and only 18 per cent in Japan and Spain. In fact, it seems that the further south you go, the less tax you pay. Looking at data from the twenty-two member countries of the Organization for Economic Cooperation and Development (OECD), we find that tax revenue as a proportion of GNP falls on average by seven percentage points for every ten degree decline in latitude. The reason behind the high taxes in countries further north lies, of course, in their extensive welfare programmes. After all, the government cannot obtain resources for free; it must pay for these resources and, ultimately, the only source of government financing is taxes. For even when the government goes into debt and borrows moneý from the public, it must pay the interest and principle on those borrowings out of tax revenues later on.

One of the most misunderstood aspects of all welfare programmes in all countries involves the system of social security. The British and Scandinavian systems are designed to cover the whole population, not just individual groups. EEC countries are moving in that direction also, but most countries on the continent traditionally run social security on occupational insurance lines. The usual pattern is for compulsory social security insurance to cover employees in business and industry to be administered by a large number of separate agencies which serve the various regions and cater to the various risks insured.

Not surprisingly, all of the faults in the American social security system seem to be recreated and even multiplied in the social security systems throughout Europe. For example, most social security systems are earnings-related and, therefore, tend to produce a high level of benefits for workers in industry, but at the expense of other groups, mainly casual workers, dependents and the self-employed. And as in the United States, the social security systems are not like private pension plans but, rather, involve mere transfers from the working people in each society to the non-working. Unfortunately, social security taxes are paid by even the lowest income-earning members of society to finance the pensions of essentially the middle class. It's not surprising that social security has been labelled a system of welfare by which the poor support the middle class.

An unusual aspect of social security is that employers' contributions are considered by most citizens to be a 'gift' paid not by the employee, but by the employer. This is indeed an unusual analysis. The employer's contribution on behalf of any employee represents a cost to the employer, just like wages, interest on loans, material expenses, and so on. The employer's contribution represents, just as the employee's, a tax on the employee, for employees' wages are effectively lowered because of the social security system. That is to say, if employers did not pay the contribution for each employee, wages would be higher.

A good part of the social security budgets in such countries as France and Belgium are paid out in the form of family allowances. In fact, in those two countries just mentioned, fully one-fifth of total social security budgets are given in the form of family allowances, which represent nearly 5 per cent of the average family's net income. Benefits depend on the number of children and on their age. They can range from £7 to £20 a month. As we noted in Chapter 3, this family allowance system is an incentive to have more children. If it were eliminated and all things remained constant, the birth rate in France would probably fall.

Another less generous form of welfare in most European countries relates to unemployment benefits. In Germany and the Benelux countries, benefits are related to earnings, being usually 60 to 90 per cent with some upper limit. France and Italy pay a flat rate to the unemployed, but in France most wage earners are covered by a supplementary insurance and therefore end up drawing between 30 to 50 per cent of their normal basic wages. A British worker on unemployment in 1973 received £6.75p a week plus earnings-related supplementary benefits. A little known aspect of this form of welfare is the incentive it gives workers to remain unemployed. After all, when a worker goes back to work, he loses his unemployment benefits, which are tax free, and starts having to pay taxes on the earnings he or she makes. It is certainly true that there would be lower rates of unemployment in all countries if unemployment insurance were eliminated. Studies done in Canada and the United States, for example, suggest that at least one and probably two full percentage *points* of total unemployment are directly caused by unemployment insurance. A new unemployment law in British Columbia, for example, required that people worked only eight weeks to be eligible for the entire year. The result was predictable but shocking. After the law was passed, hoards of them quit after eight weeks of work. At ski areas around Vancouver, British Columbia, some ambitious entrepreneurs started ski clubs where, included in the young members' payments in respect of board, lodging and a season ticket for their ski-ing, was the provision of transportation each week to the nearest benefit office for members to collect their unemployment cheques. In the logging industry, which is highly seasonal during the summer, turnover rates increased to 600 per cent because loggers quit after eight weeks to collect unemployment benefits and had a ready-made excuse for the unemployment office as to why they couldn't find other work, their excuse being that the season was almost over in logging. The same situation occurred in the highly seasonal tourist industry that employs large numbers of young people during the summers as clerks, waiters and so on.

Any analysis of welfare in any country must look at the incentive effects of various programmes. We've already discussed in Chapter 7 the incentive effects of the British National Health Service, which continues to charge a zero price for most of its services. The incentive in that system for reducing the need for medical care has been effectively lowered drastically. We also talked about the incentives implicit in the various housing policies in different countries in Chapter 2.

An alternative to the massive, complicated, and adverse incentive-inducing welfare programmes that exist throughout the world is obvious: rather than attempt to provide welfare to people in kind via unemployment insurance, family allowances, health care, housing services, etc., governments can provide those who are truly in need of assistance with the wherewithal to purchase what the individual, and not the government, deems the most desirable. This could be accomplished through a system of cash grants to people with incomes below a certain level, or by a more complicated system of what we would call a negative income tax. As people's income fell below a certain level, instead of paying taxes they would receive a payment from the government that was, say, 50 per cent of the difference between a decent or livable income and the actual income earned. In this manner, there is still an incentive not to work, but that incentive would not be as great in the situation where an outright cash grant is given to everybody earning below a minimum level. This system is under serious discussion in North America, and may be a solution to the welfare ills that plague all countries today.

Chapter 17

The Economics of Pensions

Saving for a rainy day is not an uncommon type of behaviour anywhere in the world. The form in which people save takes on many shapes: some save in piggy banks, others buy stocks and bonds, others buy property and still others stuff cash under their mattresses. The one rainy day that everybody is certain about is the day that one is too old to work and hence, must retire. Retirement is a fact of life for at least 99.99 per cent of the labour force throughout Europe and the British Isles. And, of course, when people retire, they no longer have an income stream from their work. Rather, another type of income stream must be provided. This can be in the form of income plus depreciation of principle on past accumulated savings. It can also be in the form of a pension plan. Pension plans can be provided by governments or by private organizations. Throughout the European Economic Community (EEC), retirement plans vary greatly.

In Holland, the Government aims to keep pensions in line with the minimum legal wage and pay them to everyone, whether a housewife or a managing director. Elsewhere in the EEC, pensions are based partly on the number of years insured, partly on earnings.

In France and Belgium, for example, they rise to between 50 and 75 per cent of *average* earnings. In Germany and Italy, they are calculated on the basis of final earnings. The minimum pension in 1973 ran to about £935 a year in Belgium, £410 in France, £250 in Italy, and about £350 a year for a single person or £530 for a married couple in Britain.

Whenever there is a pension scheme that provides to working individuals no longer working pensions that exceed the payments plus interest accrued paid in by those individuals the difference must be made up somewhere. Generally it is supplemented from general funds from the Exchequer. That is, it is made up of taxes paid by current working members of society. This is one aspect of national pension systems that is often overlooked. This should be contrasted to the situation of a private pension system in which the individual member cannot receive more than is put in, plus interest accrued.

Certain pension schemes are financed in very wierd ways. One French solution to the problem of paying pensions for shopkeepers had an effect that could easily be predicted. The pension would be financed by a levy on large shops. Those of 400 square metres or more would have to pay an annual tax of 15 francs per square metre. Imagine what supermarkets over 2,500 square metres would be paying. Although supermarkets account for less than 30 per cent of retail sales in France, their steady growth has reflected a definite change of French shopping habits. If, however, the pension plan financing system is to remain viable, there will obviously be a shift backward toward markets with smaller square footage. You can also imagine the incentive for owners of supermarkets to curtail expansion and to be more efficient in exhibiting goods on a vertical rather than a horizontal plane.

The levy passed in 1972 was to apply only to shops built within the last ten years. Just as in the case of employers' contributions to social security outlined in the last chapter, this particular levy will be considered another cost of doing business. And ultimately it will be reflected in lower salaries for French shopworkers and/ or higher food prices for French consumers.

As another example of unexpected but equally easily predictable results of pension system changes, we move now to Italy. In the middle of 1973, when the new Centre Left coalition Government came into office headed by Mariano Rumor, there was an exodus of half the administrative class of civil servants. They did not leave the Government because they were against the new coalition headed by Rumor; rather, they left for a much better reason. The Government presented them with a special retirement incentive plan. The incentives included a seven-year increase in seniority, pensions based on the grade *above* each civil servant's last post, and a 12.5 per cent pension increase if he or she happened to have fought in the last war. Not surprisingly, numerous bureaucrats found themselves offered pensions larger than the salaries they were earning. They'd have been stupid not to quit, and immediately 6,764 did quit, leaving behind only 5,140 colleagues to administer the entire machinery of State. A full 2,000 more than expected took their early handshake. Wouldn't you? After all, working was costly given the change in rules for pensions. And to make matters worse, many if not most civil servants got promoted, as they had in the past, one grade up just before retiring, thus getting a double last-minute promotion according to the new rules. For example, one 47-year old retired from the Ministry of Transport on 30 June 1973 with a pension corresponding to forty years' service. Within a few months, 93 per cent of the senior civil servants at the labour ministry, 89 per cent at the defence ministry, and 90 per cent at the Ministry of Tourism left. The figures were somewhat lower for Justice and Finance - 69 and 62 per cent respectively - but the results there were even more dramatic given the already incredibly slow, archaic legal and financial system that exists in that country.

In order to pay for the tremendous increases in pensions, the Government at that time instituted a new system of personal tax. Unfortunately, with over half of the Ministry of Finance's administrative class gone, there was going to be nobody to collect it!

Chapter 18

The Economics of Guest Workers

By the beginning of this decade, Germany, France, Switzerland, Benelux and the United Kingdom had almost 6 million migrant workers. Fully 28 per cent of these 6 million 'guests' were from Italy, another 15 per cent from Span, almost 10 per cent from Portugal, and the remainder from Greece, Turkey, Yugoslavia and a few other countries. The above figures leave out the guest workers that are also in Scandinavian countries and in Austria. In fact, according to some observers, the above figures for all of western Europe are decidedly too low since the UN Economic Commission for Europe put the total at 5.4 million as early as 1965. That means that the total number of migrants working in the industrialized western European countries may be about 8 million. This represents some 7 per cent of the total labour force in the recipient countries. In Switzerland, the proportion is as high as 29 per cent.

Most guest workers are male with possibly 60 per cent in the 18 to 35 age group, and 30 per cent in the 35 to 45 group. The majority of married migrants leave their families at home. For example, in 1968, 72 per cent of foreign workers in Germany were married, but only 39 per cent of these had their spouses with them.

Let's first look at why so many people have migrated to industrialized Western countries. The basic reason is not hard to figure out. A person will migrate to another country or location generally for economic reasons - to achieve a higher standard of living. A decision to migrate on purely economic grounds will include not only the potential gain in income, but also any costs involved in migration.

The most obvious cost of migration is transportation. After that is the cost of searching for a job once the migrant arrives in another country. The job search costs can be high if in fact the migrant is out of work for a long time.

Another cost to consider is the cost of setting up a new household in a different city, and dismantling the one already created in the would-be migrant's current country. Costs here are not only economic but also psychic - losing old friends and trying to make new ones, leaving relatives, and so on.

All of these costs of migration are incurred at the very beginning, so they loom larger in the would-be migrant's mind than the potential benefit of higher wages that he will obtain once he gets work in another city. In the economic decision, then, the expected or anticipated stream of *differences* in wages (because that's really what one has to look at) must be compared with the anticipated migration costs that are incurred almost immediately and which are generally of a once-and-for-all nature.

One can predict that between any two countries where earnings differentials exist, the phenomenon of migration will tend to reduce those differences over time. After all, as the supply of labour increases in the receiving company, wage rates will grow less rapidly. Whereas in the sending country, as the supply of labour falls, wage rates will grow more rapidly than they would otherwise. Some studies have been done on earnings differentials between Yugoslavia and two recipient countries, France and Germany, over the period 1960 to 1968. The results from the study confirm our predictions: the gap between earnings has narrowed for Germany and Yugoslavia, and even more so for France and Yugoslavia.

Some major contributing factors to the large amount of migration in Europe probably include but are not limited to:

1 political détente in Europe;

2 the 1957 Treaty of Rome establishing the EEC; and

3   subsequent European unification.

Moreover, there have been explicit legal and institutional arrangements designed to encourage such labour movement. Most major labour-importing countries now have well-established official recruiting institutions for migrant labour which operate through formal bilateral agreements with the sending countries.

One can view migration in western Europe as the equivalent of a huge effort in development assistance rendered by the countries receiving labour to those sending it. However, such disguised foreign aid does not come without its problems.

Since migrant workers are substitutes, in some sense for domestic workers, there is pressure to eliminate the flow of migrants, whenever the unemployment rates rise in industrialized Western countries. For example, in 1972 when the French Government was confronted by unemployment of over a half a million individuals out of jobs, it started taking a hard look at its foreign workers. At that time, immigrants numbered 3.3 million, among them mainly Algerians, Spaniards, Portuguese and Italians. At least 75 per cent of the immigrants were at that time unskilled and, according to the French Government, under-paid, under-housed, and so desperate they were willing to take jobs at much lower wage rates than Frenchmen. The French Government started putting pressure on sending countries' governments to stem the flow of migrant workers on the pretext, of course, that so many were coming in that the country could not make a 'satisfactory welcome' possible. The reason, of course, that the French Government wanted to stem the flow of foreigners was to satisfy unions in France who saw foreigners as unwelcomed individuals who reduced employment possibilities for French nationals.

Germany also has in recent years decided to stem the flow of foreigners, even when unemployment is not high. The reason, according to Government officials, is because of the difficulty of absorbing non-Germans into the society. According to Willi Brandt in the late spring of 1973: 'It has become necessary to think very carefully about the limits of our society's capacity to absorb [this flow of immigrants] and about the need for good sense and social responsibility to call a halt.' In keeping with Brandt's desire, a programme was submitted to the Cabinet to reduce the inflow. Among the possibilities was a rise in the recruitment fee that employers pay to the Federal Labour Office, which is the official German agency that brings in the bulk of workers through offices in the recruitment countries. There was also talk about a special levy on employers by local authorities to make more money available for the social services that had to be provided for immigrants. The employers, naturally, resisted this idea vigorously.

Speaking of social services for immigrants, it is interesting to note that any system which taxes employers of immigrants to pay for such things as improved living conditions and health care may in fact make guest workers worse off than better. The reasoning is not hard to follow. If the employer has to pay for expenses related to the hiring and use of immigrants, the employer will consider these taxes as part of the pay to the immigrant - i.e. as part of his labour expenses. The way employers react to such a tax is to hire fewer immigrants than they would otherwise and/or reduce the wages offered to those workers. In both cases, immigrants as a group are worse off. The people who really benefit from improved living conditions for immigrants paid for by their employers are other workers. It would not be surprising to find out that the forces behind legislation requiring that social services be provided to immigrants are all centred in the syndicates throughout industrialized Western countries.

All that seems good for the people being helped may, in fact, turn out not to be good at all.

Chapter 19

The Economics of
Discrimination and Women's Liberation

Article 119 of the Treaty of Rome stipulates that men and women should receive equal pay. For several years now, the EEC has been aware that a number of member countries have refused to live up to Article 119. For example, in the last few months of 1973, the EEC's Commission on Social Affairs asked Holland to explain why it did not have a stipulation in its national laws guaranteeing equal pay for equal work for all members of Dutch society. The Dutch were angry at the EEC's report because they argued that other member countries had just as much job discrimination, but were hiding it in better disguised official statistics. Nonetheless, crude pay figures at that time suggested that Holland had the largest wage differential for men and women of all countries in the Community.

Casual statistical observations indicate that although women make up one-third of the EEC's labour force, the percentage of total wages earned is far less than that.

The percentage of working women aged 14 to 59 ranges from the relatively high - over 50 per cent as in France - to the relatively low - under 25 per cent as in Italy. According to a study done by the French sociologist Madame Evelyne Sullerot, Community members have made an insufficient effort to provide the needed social facilities, such as creches, day nurseries, and school canteens that would enable European women to work. She also points out, interestingly enough, that laws aimed at enforcing equality and, thus, complying with Article 119, have tended to price women out of the market by requiring, for example, employers to contribute to maternity benefits.

Before we decide whether the kind of statistics that are available on the wages and working participation rates of women throughout the British Isles, Scandinavia, and continental Europe, constitute a strong case for the existence of discrimination and exploitation, we should come up with a more refined definition of what those concepts actually mean.

The everyday meaning of exploitation is simply 'not being paid enough for what you sell (labour services or goods) and having to pay too much for what you buy.' Discrimination is usually taken to mean about the same as exploitation, but may also include not being able to find work at all and not being able to buy a certain product, such as housing, in particular neighbourhoods.

The economists' definition of exploitation is somewhat more restrictive. We consider in this book that a person is being exploited in the selling of his or her labour services if he or she is being paid less than the value of his or her services. He or she is being exploited in the buying of goods and services if he or she pays a price that exceeds the (marginal) cost of the product or service he or she is buying. (Note here that cost also includes normal profits.)

Using this definition of exploitation, let's see how it is possible for this phenomenon to exist. First and foremost, lack of information allows for exploitation. When employees are ignorant of better job opportunities, they may be exploited by employers. When consumers are unaware of other and cheaper product sources, they may be exploited by sellers.

Restricted entry is another cause of exploitation. If a food merchant in an isolated town successfully prevents entry by new firms, consumers can be forced to pay him monopoly rents over and above the competitive price for food.

A third cause of exploitation is restricted mobility. If a doctor is prevented from practicing in other than the country where he now works, he may be exploited because he is not allowed to go where the value of his services is highest (and so, too, his potential income).

It should be noted that each of the last three paragraphs included the phrase 'may be exploited'. Stress is placed on the 'may'. The lack of information, free entry, and mobility does not *prima facie* indicate exploitation. More is needed; all employees or consumers concerned must be unaware of the facts, not just the average employee or consumer.

Turning now to the more specific case where women receive generally less than men for apparently the same work, we ask the question: 'Can we sympathize with women's liberation?' The answer is not as easy as some would have us think. An objective response must take into account all factors which influence productivity and hence the amount employees in a competitive system are willing to pay female workers. But even before considering differences in productivity, we must first consider how the statistics are compiled.

We find, for example, that women are found in disproportionately large numbers in those jobs where the work is low-paid and the output of low value. The most obvious of these jobs is house-cleaning, waiting on diners in restaurants, and other so-called women's work. This is one very good reason why we do not observe women earning their fair share of total payment to the labour force. Of course, we have not explained why women do these jobs in larger numbers than men. We might hypothesize that less human capital in the form of higher education has historically been vested in women. Thus, as a group they are forced to take on lower-paid jobs which require less educational background. If true, this fact does not constitute a case of discrimination against women in the labour market *per se.* Rather, it represents historical discrimination against women in the market for education. (We note in passing that there really is no true market in education as there is a market in other areas because education has been taken over for the most part by the State.)

We might also hope to find a reason for the distribution of occupations among women being different than among men in certain sociological factors that some researchers have chosen to call role playing. It may be surprising that women's work is not the same in other countries. For example, in Africa heavy physical labour is regarded as women's work whereas we certainly cannot maintain the same for Europe. Also, women's work in Russia involves sweeping the streets, in Asia tilling the fields, and so on. In Europe not even 10 per cent of the doctors are women, but in Russia women constitute more than three-quarters of all doctors. While Women's Liberation may decry role differentiation as it now stands in the Western world, this cultural problem has nothing whatsoever to do with the commonly accepted notion of employer discrimination in the job market.

What about less pay for equal work for women? Does the fact that women in the same occupation as men earn less on average indicate the presence of discrimination? Certainly this may be so, but again we are not sure. We know that employers take into account many factors while making their hiring and firing decisions and also in deciding on the wages offered. Discrimination may be one of these, but the data do not indicate with certainty that it is the most important. Employers are confronted with the problem of minimization of costs, and they realize that all new employees must be trained on the job to some extent. On-the-job training, while differing in different situations, does, though, require the employer's use of real resources - money. When the employer has the new worker learning on the job, the new worker obviously cannot produce as effectively as older workers. This is one reason why we find newly-hired workers earning wages so much less than those of workers who have already been on the job for some time. In general, the starting wage is not so low as to compensate the employer completely for all of the costs involved in training the new worker. Hence, the employer makes an investment in every worker whom he employs. If the employer wishes to maximize the return from this investment, he will take into account the historical information available on individuals applying for jobs and on the class of individuals he is looking at. If, historically, women are less apt to stay on the job as long as men, then many employers will tend to hire fewer women if given two applicants with equal qualifications except for differences in sex.

Now, we are not necessarily concerned with absenteeism and length of stay on a particular job. Recent data have shown that women in certain industries stay on the job as long as men. But we know that the labour participation rate of women is lower than men and more highly fluctuating. That is, women tend to leave the labour force for long periods more often than men. Also employers are usually adept enough at distinguishing between the participation rates of single women as opposed to married women. At about thirty-five years of age the average single woman remains in her job for about thirty more years. That is, at thirty-five her work life expectancy is more than thirty years. Her married counterpart, though, will only have a work-life expectancy of less than twenty-five years.

Since Women's Liberation has not been established long enough to provide sufficient data as a basis for objective assessment, we cannot yet discuss how much of the income differential between men and women is due to male chauvinism. We are suggesting that more work of the nature described above should be done in order to establish the actual measure of whatever discrimination that does exist.

Chapter 20

The Economics of Crime

Estimates of total losses in the United Kingdom from shoplifting and staff thefts vary from under £200 million to over £500 million a year. There has been a sharp increase in many countries in crimes of violence against a person. If one were to compile the total number of murders, rapes, muggings, robberies, etc. throughout Scandinavia, the British Isles, and the EEC, the rate of increase would be staggering, and quite frightening. This is not the place for us to try to explain the sociological reasons behind criminal activity. We can, however, come up with some notions about how crime can be prevented and what determines the supply of criminal activity.

Some people believe that the more money spent on crime deterrence, the less crime there will be. However, it is not known what relationship there is between money spent on deterrence and the actual number of crimes that are not committed because of that spending. It takes an extremely clever pollster to discover how many times an individual *didn't* break the law. We are even less certain about the effectiveness of the different methods used to deter crime. Is it best to have policemen everywhere? Or, is it best to have a system of paid informants in lieu of those policemen? Should we allow innocent parties to be apprehended and prosecuted merely because a larger absolute number of the guilty will thereby be convicted? We also have to think about the available alternatives to punishing guilty offenders. Should we allow for large fines instead of incarceration? Should we have public whippings? Should capital punishment be allowed? In terms of establishing a system of crime deterrence, we might want to assess carefully the value of different methods of supposed deterrents.

Let's look at the reasoning. All decisions are made on the margin. If an act of theft will be punished by hanging and an act of murder will be punished by the same fate, there is no marginal deterrence to murder. If a theft of £5 is met with a punishment of ten years in gaol and a theft of £50,000 also incurs a ten-year sentence, then why not steal £50,000? Why not go for the £50,000? There is no marginal deterrence to prevent one from doing so.

A very serious question exists as to how our system of justice can establish penalties which are appropriate from a social point of view. To establish the correct (marginal) deterrences, we must observe empirically how criminals respond to changes in punishments. This leads us to the question of how people decide whether to commit a 'crime'. A theory needs to be established as to what determines the supply of criminal offences.

Adam Smith once said:

The affluence of the rich excites the indignation of the poor, who are often both driven by want, and prompted by envy, to invade his possessions. It is only under the shelter of the civil magistrate that the owner of that valuable property, which is acquired by the labour of many years, or perhaps by many successive generations, can sleep a single night in security. He is at all times surrounded by unknown enemies, whom, though he never provokes, he can never appease, and from whose injustice he can be protected only by the powerful arm of the civil magistrate continually held up to chastise it. The acquisition of valuable and extensive property, therefore, necessarily requires the establishment of civil government. Where there is no property, or at least none that exceeds the value of two or three days' labour, civil government is not so necessary. *

---

*Adam Smith, *The Wealth of Nations*, 1776

Smith is pointing out that the professional criminal is looking for income. If he is looking for income, then his decision-making process could be looked at like any other. He looks at the expected returns and expected costs of criminal activity. He then compares them with the net returns from legitimate activities. The costs of crime involve apprehension, defence, conviction, gaol, and so on.

Viewing the supply of offences thus, we can come up with methods by which society can lower the net expected rate of return for committing any illegal activity. That is, we can figure out how to reduce crime most effectively. We have talked about one particular aspect - the size of penalties. We also briefly mentioned the other - i.e. the probability of detection for each offence. When either of these costs of crime goes up, the supply of offences goes down; i.e. less crime is committed.

How can the probability of detection be increased? There are numerous methods - increased police activity being only one. Individuals can privately increase the probability of detecting people attempting to rob their homes. The market for individual burglar alarm systems is a burgeoning one indeed. There are also varied amounts of technologically sophisticated equipment that can be used to increase detection and apprehension. Wire-tapping is one of them. This approach, however, presents a problem of infringing individual liberties - a cost which must be reckoned with whenever it is used. It is also possible for certain 'traps' to be set up so as to apprehend more criminals. For example, if money were made in a much more complicated manner, it would be more difficult for counterfeiters to copy it successfully and go undetected.

The probability of conviction is very important in increasing the net expected cost of committing an illegal activity. This involves our legal system, which today is in a sorry state. If a person knows that even if he is apprehended, he will not be convicted, then of course the expected cost to him of comitting a crime is decreased. The likelihood of conviction is apparently an important factor in the presentation of crime. Currently, the probability of conviction for a crime is quite low in, for example, the United States. In New York City it is estimated that a man who commits a felony faces less than one chance in two hundred of going to gaol. One major reason for this is because the Courts lack adequate facilities to handle the large number of cases seeking admission to them. The Court calendars in many cities are clogged beyond belief: many are booked for two, three, or even four years into the future. The average time lapse between filing a civil suit and getting it to trial is forty months in New York City. What do you think happens? An overworked prosecuting attorney and his team of crime-busting assistants increasingly have to arrange pre-trial settlements rather than put an additional weight on the already over-burdened Courts. Eighty to 90 per cent of criminal charges are settled before trial. Money might be spent better on streamlining Court proceedings than on making more arrests. The district attorneys would not be forced to make so many 'deals' with suspects. There are, of course, many inequities on the other side of the coin.

Obviously it is difficult to assess the social value that people in general place on the prevention of different types of crime. Police and Government officials certainly have a hard time figuring out how resources should be expended in the different areas of criminal deterrence. There is a possibility, though, of improving the information being used by different decision-makers. Currently there is almost no compensation to the victim or to his or her dependents in the case of violent crime. If you were knocked over the head on the street by a robber, you would probably try to sue him if he is apprehended. But in most cases you certainly wouldn't get much money. If somebody is supporting you and that person is killed or maimed by a crazy gangster, you as the dependent would be able to collect nothing from the gangster or the Government. In fact, you would probably end-up paying because the criminal might be apprehended and sent to gaol. You would end up paying for his care while he was in gaol.

A possible solution which might improve the allocation of resources in a more economically efficient direction is the following: individual local authorities could assume responsibility for complete liability of anyone within their geographical territory. If the unlimited liability were assessed against the State in the case of criminal assaults and crimes against property, then the taxpayers would find a portion of their taxes going to compensate victims of crimes. This would eventually come back through the political process as a demand for better law enforcement in those areas that were most expensive to taxpayers. Most likely, fewer resources would be spent on apprehending and convicting victimless criminals, such as prostitutes and marijuana smokers, and more resources would be spent on preventing robberies, assaults, rapes and murders. We would expect a more optimal allocation of resources to prevail within police departments. Also, there may be an effort to streamline the Courts in order to increase the probability of conviction. Further, our prisons may be turned into rehabilitation institutions instead of schools for improved criminal activities which increase future crime.

Chapter 21

The Economics of Traffic Jams

In 1960, the world had about thirty-five cars per thousand people. At that time, Britain had about 110 per thousand, France a little more, with Germany somewhat below a hundred, and Italy at around forty-five per thousand. An OECD forecast for 1980 projects that the total world car population will rise to seventy per thousand people, with Germany, France, Britain and Italy all around 350 per thousand. Cars are engulfing us, everywhere and in every way. Cities are becoming masses of congested streets and filled parking lots.

To drive a car into central London, Copenhagen, Stockholm, Munich, Amsterdam or Paris - just to take a few examples - at the rush hour of a mid-week evening is to court frustration and delay. The same holds for just about any big city in the world. Congestion is a problem that is sometimes overwhelming. You can do absolutely nothing when you get stuck in your car in a traffic jam. You can abandon your car (and then get fined), but otherwise you're stuck.

In most cities congestion is a problem that occurs only during selected hours of the day. You can, most likely, drive anywhere you want at three o'clock in the morning in any city in the world without running into traffic problems. The problem of congestion usually limits itself to peak periods of street use. It is a peak-loading problem, where the system is overloaded during the morning and afternoon rush hours. And there doesn't seem to be much incentive on the part of the individual drivers to change the situation.

When somebody enters his car to take a drive in the city at rush hour, he incurs the private costs of driving - the cost of petrol, oil, maintenance, insurance and so on. He also incurs a time cost; the longer he is held up in traffic, the more expensive it becomes to drive. The time cost is directly related to the driver's opportunity cost. It is more expensive for a £20,000 a year busy executive to get stuck in central London than it is for a £15 a week clerk. The executive's opportunity cost is much higher than the clerk's. This does not mean, of course, that they both won't become equally annoyed.

There are other costs that our driver creates but does not incur. There is the cost to other drivers caused by him slowing them down. If traffic is moving smoothly but one additional car causes a tie-up, then the driver of that additional car imposes a time cost on everybody else. Additionally, he imposes costs on all those who want to drive but don't because they know the streets will be congested. As yet there is no way people can bribe this driver to stay off the road so they can drive without congestion. Nor can he offer to stay off the streets. A contract would be difficult to create and to enforce. This question raises the issue of whether there's a way out of this dilemma. Is there a way to make private costs equal to social costs? There is, and it is called peak-load pricing.

Let's take the example of a toll bridge that goes into a city. It is crowded perhaps four hours of each day. During that time cars creep along at 10 km/hour taking a half-hour to cross the bridge. The non-peak crossing time is ten minutes. This is a typical peak-load problem. The bridge is uncrowded during the rest of the day. The next question is whether there are ways to discourage people from using the bridge during peak periods. One way involves a surcharge, or an additional charge, for use during that time. In this manner, drivers would be faced with a truer representation of the marginal cost of using the bridge during peak periods. That marginal cost involves preventing other drivers from getting on to the bridge and slowing down those already on it. Toll bridges, however, are usually not priced in this manner.

Usually, exactly the opposite occurs in most cities that have toll bridges. Instead of charging a higher price during peak periods, a lower price is charged by way of special commuter tickets that are lower priced than the regular tickets. Commuter tickets are mainly purchased by businessmen and workers who use the bridge exactly at peak hours. This is an example of *reverse* peak-load pricing. If we assume that the responsiveness of demand for the services of the bridge is not completely zero, a decrease in the price encourages more use. We therefore have more people on the bridge at peak periods than we would have if we had no system of lower-priced commuter tickets. On the other hand, you can be sure that if the price for peak-time use of the bridge were raised sufficiently, there would be no peak-period problem. Commuters would start using more car pools. Some central businesses would find it advantageous to allow their employees to come and leave at other than the normal periods, thereby saving their employees the peak-period price on the bridge. People casually going into the city over the bridge would alter their schedules so as to avoid peak periods. In other words, there would be a change in the transportation habits of those who used the bridge.

You might be upset by the thought of charging a higher price to commuters who have to come at peak periods because you might maintain that they are the ones least able to afford the penalty fee. That, in fact, may be true. Remember, though, that the higher peak-load price is really a reflection of the true, higher social marginal cost of using the bridge during the rush hour. At any rate, it is difficult to find out what people can really afford, which is not the issue here anyway. We are discussing methods of eliminating congestion around our urban areas, and our object is to discover the optimal use of resources. Here the resource in question happens to be a bridge. A peak-load pricing system will discourage use of the bridge during peak periods. If you think that some people will not be able to afford the increase in price, then you are really concerned about the current distribution of income - which is a separate issue from the allocation of resources.

Other solutions have been suggested by various groups throughout the world. A study by the Greater London Council suggested, for example, that parking be phased out within the city to discourage people from coming into it. Another suggestion was supplementary licensing; anybody who wanted to drive in the central area at busy times of the day would have to buy a second licence, the price of which would be pitched quite high. This would discourage residents from owning any car at all. Other possibilities include a total ban on traffic, which has been done in Venice (eliciting complaints about congested canals) and in small towns like Zermatt. A less draconian solution is to limit traffic to certain streets. Sometimes the benefits of this limitation seem to over-whelm the costs. For example, when the main road between Windsor and Eton had to be closed because the narrow Thames bridge linking them was damaged, the County Council decided not to re-open the bridge for motor traffic because people enjoyed a car-free atmosphere so much. Hamburg has cut-off several square miles to traffic, and to compensate for this, it has opened one of the most efficient public transport systems in the world. The London Oxford Street experience, where buses and taxis only are there for certain times of the day, is a variant of the Hamburg solution, and it is being extended to neighbouring streets.

Of course, the major drawback of these kinds of traffic control systems is that they merely shift the problem somewhere else. So long as people are not forced to pay the full social cost of driving their cars, there is going to be a problem of 'too' many cars in any one city during its rush hour. Mass transit is not a solution unless the true cost of driving is presented to the motor-car owner, for people like to drive into town even in traffic jams, since their cars are more comfortable, convenient, weather-proof, and private than any form of public transport.

There are ways to economize on the use of private cars, and one would be for more people to crowd into each car. That is, people could be encouraged to use car pools, thereby eliminating a certain number of cars at rush hours. One way of doing this is by fining all drivers in certain multi-lane highways who do not have at least two other people in their car. In the same vein, but in the opposite direction, we could allow cars filled with, say, three or more people to get a reduced price for toll roads and toll bridges. This has been used in California's San Francisco Golden Gate Bridge: cars with four or more people drive over it in a special toll-free lane. One would be surprised at how many car pools are springing up in San Francisco to take advantage of this reward system.

The problems surrounding the use of cars throughout the world seem overwhelming, but they are far from insurmountable. A little rational pricing of scarce resources might help quite a bit.

Chapter 22

The Economics of Supersonic
Transportation

When Harold Wilson's Labour Government first took office in 1964, it immediately attempted to cancel the Anglo-French airliner, the Concorde. A decade later in 1974, Tony Wedgewood-Benn, then Secretary of State for Industry in the new Wilson minority Government, even though regarding himself as a Concorde partisan, gave Parliament facts that suggested that the cheapest thing to do with the Concorde would be to scrap it. By March of 1974, firm sales had only totalled nine, all to Concorde's captive, State-owned customers, British Airways and Air France. The facts about the Concorde are quite startling in and of themselves, but some of the implications of that project are even more so, as we will see in a moment.

During the first ten or so years of the Concorde's development, something over £1 billion in development costs had been expended. The mounting production costs in the Concorde are, of course, well known to everyone. What may not be understood is that there is no way that the Concorde could be produced and sold that would recoup any of the losses already sustained.

In economics, generally, or in business more specifically, that which occurred in the past has already occurred; i.e. sunk costs can never be recouped. All of the developmental expenses that have gone into the Concorde should have no effect on the decision whether or not to continue development and/or production. In the private enterprise operation, the decision to go ahead on a project is based on the future profitability, not the past. It is, of course, painful to scrap a project that has cost over £1 billion, but the taxpayer in both Britain and France will certainly be better off. For if a hundred Concordes are built and sold, the British share alone of the production *losses* might reach £1 to £3 million.

It is surprising that the cancellation of the American SST aircraft

did not encourage one bit the people in charge of using public
monies to continue development of the Anglo-French version. It
might be instructive to look at the arguments that were used for
and against the American SST to see if in fact they apply to the
Concorde.

A few years ago when the debate was raging in the Congress of the
United States, private airlines, as they all are in that country,
weren't absolutely sure they would buy the SST right away, but
they knew that at some time in the future profits would be higher
if the SSTs were around. They certainly weren't unwilling to have
the Government build the SST at public expense. And, in fact,
they lobbied for such a Government activity, using reasoning that
would make most logicians cry.

One representative of a large American aircraft manufacturer
indicated that building the SST would promote international
understanding. He also indicated that the sales of the United
States SST would generate tax dollars to fight all the social ills in
that country, indicating that if there were no support for the SST,
social problems of the future would be even worse. The fallacy in
such an argument was obvious: if in fact there were social
problems that could be solved by Government aid, the Americans
could have taken the $2 billion that was at that time scheduled
to be spent on the SST project and help out those in need directly.

The environmentalists who were against the project pointed out
some environmental problems. The din from a normal jet is
nothing compared to that of the SST. The bang zone of the SST
sonic boom is about fifty miles, or 75 kilometres. That's only the
width. The length is the entire length of supersonic flight - 3,000
to 5,000 kilometres. It has been calculated that if overland sonic
transport is permitted, there would be a boom in every room for
those unlucky 500 million people in the world within the bang

zone of all the passing SSTs.

Environmentalists also point out that the noise problem wasn't the only thing that could be expected from SST travel. They claim that it will increase the water vapour content of the stratosphere, leading to climatic changes that will do harm to the environment. Also, the amount of hydrocarbons released in the air would be enormous.

None of these questions seem to be argued any more about the Concorde. However, one aspect of its continued development and production is important to note, even if it is ignored.

The Concorde, just like luxury liners such as *Le France*, is a prestige activity that involves enormous costs. Who benefits from these prestige activities? They directly serve a small class of high-income individuals, and most of those high-income individuals will not be British or French, but rather foreigners. In other words, 95 per cent or more of the British and French populations will be paying large sums to provide a supersonic transport that will benefit 5 per cent or less of those respective populations. A better figure would be 99.9999 per cent of the populations subsidize the remainder. In spite of such an obvious fact, the French Communist Party came out in 1974 against the termination of both the Concorde project and the luxury liner *Le France*. The argument was that there would be tremendous amounts of jobs lost if those two programmes were collapsed. However, what the Communist Party did not understand was the fact that the money released from those two projects in both Britain and France could be used for something else, thus creating jobs elsewhere. Moreover, if the job argument had any validity, which it generally doesn't, it would indicate that Government spending could create jobs at will. If that were the case, why couldn't Government spending be used to prevent all unemployment at any time in any country in the world?

What can we conclude, then? We can conclude that a project such as the Concorde is a method by which a very small fraction of the citizens of the countries involved receive benefits paid for by the rest of the citizens. There are other areas in which public funds can be expended which might have fewer such undesired distribution effects, and also might have higher value to society. The construction of a SST such as the Concorde, which has cost literally billions of pounds and will never turn a profit, is tantamount to a waste of scarce resources. The reason that private industry never wanted to undertake a supersonic airliner till now is because, privately, such an aircraft would not be profitable. That means that the value to society of its services is less than the cost of providing them. Generally this calls for the non-development of such a project.

Chapter 23

The Economics of Cod

A few years ago, Iceland decided that its coastal waters were being 'over-fished' by British, West German, and other foreign trawlers. So it imposed a fifty-mile territorial limit around its island. The fifty-mile limit immediately angered British fishermen, and they decided to ignore Iceland's proclamation.

So started the well-known Cod War that was raging in 1973 and 1974. While Iceland's gunboats were firing live rounds across foreign trawlers' bows and Iceland's seamen were attempting to board foreign fishing boats, governments around the world started taking a closer look at the 'outrageous' act of extending territorial waters past existing limits. It was not surprising that while the Cod War was raging, the fourteen-nation East Atlantic Fisheries Commission vetoed a proposal to fix international quotas for the fish catches on banks outside the twelve-mile territorial limits established around most countries.

To understand why there are so many problems of over-fishing in the world today, we have to take a good look at commercial ventures in that area.

On most of the high seas, there is no ownership. That is, ocean waters are generally common property and are at one and the same time owned by no one and owned by everyone. This has serious implications for the way people treat that particular natural resource.

Many people in the world like to eat fish, and many depend on fish for the basic protein element in their diet. The incentive therefore is existent for entrepreneurs to take to the seas to satisfy this recognized demand for the product of the seas.

Every individual boat owner or owner of a fishing fleet will attempt to make as much profit as possible. If you let him, he will

fish 'too much' out of any stretch of water. After all, why should
he care about the long-run consequences of all boat owners acting
just the way he does? If he slows down on the take, some other
more 'greedy' or non-conservationist-minded fisherman will be
able to get more fish and, hence, more profits.

One way to induce fishermen to act in a manner that is more
conducive to the welfare of the entire world population which
depends on fish as the protein source would be to remove the
common property aspect of ocean waters. That is to say, one
alternative to the current 'fish as much as you can and to hell with
the future' attitude of various fishing fleets is to extend private
property rights to ocean waters.

Vesting property rights in ocean waters would have been a losing
proposition a hundred years ago; it would have been impossible to
police one's property. However, things have changed, and we now
have relatively cheap electronic sensing equipment which can be
used to police large areas of water to ensure that property rights
are not violated. In fact, the problem of vanishing fish species
could be solved by parcelling out the ocean's water to various
countries. These countries would therefore have property rights in
specific locations and there would be no common-property
problem.

We would still be faced with migrating fish species, but they can
be fairly easily monitored nowadays. That means that we could
alternatively vest the property rights in specific species where
they spawned or where they were at a certain time of year. People
would buy and sell property rights in fish so that we would be
ensured that they would not be treated as a common property.
There would be no problem of over-fishing because owners of
the fishing rights would want to ensure the future of their
profitable piece of property. They would not allow over-fishing

as is done today.

Today, nations resort to a mass of artificial restrictions on the efficiency of fishermen in order to ensure that not too large a catch is taken out. That is how nations attempt to maintain the existence of any given species of fish. Now some countries, including Iceland, Ecuador and Peru, have decided that they are not going to allow over-fishing by other countries' vessels. Peru and Ecuador went to even greater 'absurdities' than Iceland by establishing 200-mile property right limits on water surrounding their shore lines. Most countries, did not, and may still not, have recognized the 200-mile limit. In fact, only the internationally recognized twelve-mile limit has been considered legal. We should note, though, that the extension of property rights to ocean waters is probably one of the most fruitful lines of endeavour that can be used to solve the problems of the conservation of aquatic species. That is how we will ensure that the future of most of the world's aquatic population will not be one of total extinction. While it certainly seems unfair for Iceland to eliminate the freedom of the seas around its shores because British fishermen, as well as many other nations' fishermen, have always fished there, what Iceland is doing should be taken as a signal for all other countries. Eventually, all of the fishing waters will be owned by one or more countries. We can foresee a world where fish will be harvested according to decisions made on the basis of the long-run viability of each species as compared with the short-run demands by the world population for this source of protein.

Chapter 24

The Economics of Pollution

When Samuel Taylor Coleridge visited Cologne, he counted seventy-two different stenches and wrote, 'The River Rhine, it is well known, doth wash your city of Cologne; but tell me Nymphs, what power divine shall henceforth wash the River Rhine?'

Governments throughout Europe have continually met to figure out the answer to Coleridge's query, for the River Rhine is just one smelly example of what can happen when a natural resource is treated as if it were a sewer. Among the various meetings that have taken place was one in The Hague in October 1972 where it was decided to check the dumping of salt into the river, which was ravaging Dutch farmland in the Rhine basin. By 1975, an alternative dumping scheme was to have been put into operation. The salt, by the way, had been coming from the French mines in Alsace.

Other meetings resulted in proposals to stop the dumping of chemical pollutants and the limitation of other types of pollution that would be put into the Rhine river.

Government surveys of river pollution in England and Wales resulted in proposals to spend millions and millions of pounds of public money on water and sewer services. The same has and continues to happen in every country throughout Scandinavia, Europe and the rest of the world. The Treaty of Rome even indicated some common pieces of pollution prevention legislation that should be adopted. The question to be answered is: why, in the 1970s, has pollution, be it in rivers, the air, or elsewhere, become such a problem and has warranged governmental action in all countries? Before we can understand what economists have to say about this issue, we must establish why some economic agents i.e. those causing pollution - can do harm to our environment without paying for the consequences. And the way we can understand this is by looking at the distinction between social and private costs.

When a businessman has to pay wages to workers, he knows exactly what his labour costs are. When he has to buy materials or build a plant, he knows quite well what it will cost him. When an individual has to pay for fixing his car, or pay for a pair of shoes, or for a theatre ticket, he knows exactly what the cost will be. These very explicit costs are what we term private costs. Private costs are those borne solely by the individuals who incur them. They are internal in the sense that the firm or household must explicitly take account of them.

What about a situation where a businessman can dump the waste products from his production process into a nearby river? Or what about instances where an individual can litter a public park or beach? Obviously, a cost is involved in these actions. When the businessman pollutes the water, people downstream suffer the consequences. They drink the polluted water and swim and bathe in it. They're also unable to catch as many fish as before because of the pollution. In the case of littering, the people who bear the costs are those who come along after our litter-bug has cluttered the park or the beach. The scenery certainly will be less attractive. We see that the costs of these actions are borne by people other than those who commit the actions. That is to say, the creator of the cost is not the bearer. The costs are not internalized; they are external. When we add external costs to internal or private costs, we come up with social costs. They are called social costs because society in general bears the costs and not just the individuals who create them. Pollution problems and, indeed, all problems pertaining to the environment may be viewed as situations where social costs are different than the private costs. Since some economic agents don't pay the full social costs of their actions, but rather only the smaller private costs, their actions are socially excessive.

Let's ask ourselves why the air in cities is so polluted from car exhaust fumes. When car drivers step into their cars, they bear only the private costs of driving. That is, they must pay for the petrol, oil, maintenance, depreciation, and insurance on their cars. However, they cause an additional cost - that of air pollution - which they are not forced to take account of when they make the decision to drive. The air pollution created by car exhaust gases is a social cost which, as yet, individuals do not bear directly. The social cost of driving includes all the private costs plus the cost of air pollution which society bears. Decisions that are made on the basis of private costs only will lead to too much motoring or, alternatively, too little money spent on the reduction of pollution by motor cars.

When private costs differ from social costs, we usually term the situation 'a problem of externals' because individual decision-makers are not internalizing all of the costs which society is bearing. Rather, some of these costs are remaining external to the decision-making process.

We can see here an easy method of reducing the amount of pollution and environmental degradation that now exists. Somehow the signals in the economy must be changed so that decision makers will take into account all the costs of their actions. In the case of pollution by motor-cars, we might want to devise some method whereby motorists were taxed according to the amount of pollution they caused. In the case of a firm, we might want to devise some system whereby businessmen were taxed according to the amount of pollution they were responsible for. In this manner, they would have an incentive to install pollution abatement equipment.

When you think about it, however, it may not be appropriate to levy a uniform tax according to physical quantities of pollution. After all, we're talking about social costs. Such costs are not necessarily the same everywhere in the world for the same action. If you drive your smelly belching car in the middle of a desert, you will probably not inflict any damage on anyone else. No one will be there to complain; the natural cleansing action of the large body of air around you will eliminate the pollution you generate to such an extent that it creates no economic harm. If a business-man pollutes the water in a lake that is used by no one except him and the lake is, in fact, inaccessible to everyone except him, the *economic* damage he creates by polluting it may be negligible.

Essentially, we must establish the size of the economic damages rather than the size of the physical amount of pollution. A polluting electric steam generating plant in London will cause much more damage than the same plant in, say, Nowhere, Wales. This is so because the concentration of people in London is much higher than in Nowhere. There are already innumerable demands on the air in London so that the pollution from smokestacks will not naturally be cleansed away. There are millions of people who will breathe that smelly air and thereby incur the costs of sore throats, sickness, emphysema and even early death. There are many, many buildings which will become dirtier faster because of the pollution, and many more cars and clothes will also become much dirtier. The list goes on and on, but it should be obvious that a given quantity of pollution will cause more harm in concentrated urban environments than it will in less dense rural environments. If we were to establish some form of taxation in order to align social costs with private costs and force people to internalize externalities, we would somehow have to come up with a measure of economic costs instead of physical quantities.

Is it too late? Are we already heading for disaster? Or can we assume that somehow pollution abatement will turn the tide and allow us in the future, or at least our children or grandchildren, to live in a cleaner environment? Apparently we have indeed not gone too far. We can improve our environment, but it does take resources, and we will have to spend part of our income in the process. A clean environment can be treated just like any other good or service. Presumably there is a collective demand for a cleaner environment and there is a collective supply. At a higher price, a clean environment is less desired than at a lower price. The cost of cleaning the environment seems to rise. We would expect that if somehow an optimum solution were reached, we would still have some pollution in the air and in the water, but it would be the quantity desired by the public. We would have a certain level of pollution clean-up demanded by the public at the price the public had to pay. Again, this may be upsetting to some people who wish to see our environment perfectly cleaned up. But that would be prohibitively expensive, and not many people are willing to pay the costs. They would rather live in a not-so-perfect environment and have that extra income to spend on other things. We can't simultaneously have a perfectly clean environment and the current amount of goods and services that we consume because at any moment in time we are faced with a fixed amount of resources. Environmental clean-up involves a trade-off with other goods. We see that scarcity follows us wherever we go.

Chapter 25

The Economics of Wedlock

Marriage is a contract. To what extent can we gain insights into it from economic analysis? Almost a century ago Frederick Engels maintained that monogamous marriage as it had developed in the West was little more than a contractual system whereby men exploited women.* This is hardly the revolutionary conclusion in the 1970s that it was in 1884. But whatever the current state of marriage, Engels' analysis did shed some light on its historical origins. An even clearer historical case of the contractual nature of marriage characterized traditional China. Since this Oriental system is in sharp contrast to the way marriage developed in the West, it offers some suggestive insights into an interesting but neglected aspect of economic analysis - property rights in people.

Our most recent experience, at least in the West, is that more and more marriage contracts are instituted by the individuals themselves without the aid of their parents. Indeed, nowadays it is sometimes against the will of parents, rather than with their blessing, that a marriage contract is consummated. But previous to such 'disrespectful' behaviour on the part of children, we were accustomed in the West to the prospective bride's father putting up a dowry in order to marry off his daughter. In fact, the dictionary definition of dowry is 'the money, goods, or estate that a woman brings to her husband in marriage'. In traditional China, however, the dowry is not a positive sum paid to the potential husband; rather, it is *negative*. The groom's parents put up a dowry to pay to the bride's parents. How do we explain this? Why has marriage in the Western world involved a positive dowry, but in China a negative one? Is it that a bride is worth less in the

---

*Frederick Engels, *The Origins of the Family, Private Property, and the State* International Publishers, New York, 1970.

West than in the East? Are brides' parents richer than grooms' parents in the West and not in the East? These are possible explanations, but there is a better one, which involves the stark reality of the position of women in traditional China.

The heads of families in China have held the title to all family property. Children were considered property, and there were explicit, firmly-recognized property rights vested in the heads of families for all the children. Now consider that parents, given whatever level of love and affection they might obtain from family members, might want to extract as large an income yield as possible from those family members. That is, given that parents owned their children, how could they reap the highest possible income from those children? This notion still has meaning in some countries of the world. Children are seen as income-producing assets because, in fact, they do produce income for the family.

Since in China parents had complete property rights in their children, it was the parents who participated in the marriage contract. The children could say nothing. Every marriage was a transfer of property rights from the bride's parents to the groom's parents. Obviously, the bride's parents would have to be compensated for the loss of an income-producing asset - in this instance, a daughter. This is why the dowry in traditional China has been negative.

What would determine the price of a bride in traditional China? For one thing, the groom's parents would be willing to pay more for a piece of property that could be easily controlled. In other words, if the probability of the bride's running away were reduced, the groom's parents would be willing to pay more for her. Accordingly, we find an emphasis placed on total loyalty to a husband and his parents. One custom that could prove to enhance a bride-price further by reducing the possibility of the bride's running away was the practice of foot binding. While it is often thought that foot binding was effected in order to enhance a woman's physical beauty, we here offer an alternative explanation: women with abnormally small feet have less chance of escaping!

Another way to reduce the possibility of a bride's running away from the marriage situation - and thus lowering the income-producing potential of the family unit - was to have her enter the groom's household many years before she actually married a particular family member. This, too, was a common custom. The groom's parents purchased a bride at infancy, raised her in the family unit, monitored her training, and instilled in her the desired sense of family loyalty and loyalty to her future husband. Because the groom's parents paid for the rearing of the daughter-in-law from childhood, the negative dowry for a bride purchased in infancy would have to be much lower than for a grown bride. The price would also be less than that paid for a grown-up bride because of the very high mortality rate for infants in traditional China. Finally, the price for a minor bride could be less because the productive potential of an infant was less certain than that of a grown woman.

Parents' quest to minimize the costs of carrying out a marriage contract led them to another curious habit that has long since disappeared in most societies: the so-called 'blind marriage'. The excited groom is allowed to see his bride's face for the first time only after the marriage ceremony. Why should this have anything to do with the cost of effecting the marrage contract? Well, what if sons had the notion that love and physical attractiveness are important? These uneconomical desires might come into conflict with the wealth-maximizing goals of the parents.

Traditional Chinese families were not necessarily made up of one man and one wife. Concubinage was customary, for restricting marriage to a one-to-one situation would have been inconsistent with any parent's desire to increase the household's living standard. Concubines were purchased, and, like the wife, they had a contract with the husband. Certain rights were excluded to the concubine, but most were not. Under the system of concubinage, some men had many mates and others had none. In turn, an unrestricted prostitution market was designed to meet the sexual demands of bachelors.*

Even today we may be able to explain some sociological phenomena in other countries by relatively-high bride prices. For example, in many Moslem countries homosexuality is common. Perhaps the major economic cause is a bride-price which appears, in some cases, to be five times the average annual income. Given the relative scarcity of brides, which causes their high bride-price, a lower quantity is demanded. There is a substitute for a marriage contract that does not involve the purchase of a bride, and that is homosexuality.

We can explain the variation in bride-prices in some Moslem countries not only by a woman's physical attractiveness and child-bearing potential but also by her expected economic productivity. In Afghanistan, for example, a female weaver can bring a large income to a family unit. Afghan rugs sell for £100 to £200 to tourists in the capital city. A female weaver's family could capitalize her earnings into a bride-price. The potential buyer

---

*Prostitution differed from marriage and concubinage mainly in that it involved the flexibility of a short-term rental agreement.

would have to consider in his own calculations the present value of the bride's economic potential, as he would have to wait for the rugs to be made - sometimes one to two years. We would expect, then, that the introduction of high-speed weaving machines in Moslem countries would lead to a reduction in the price of hand-woven rugs and, hence, a reduction in the bride-price for Moslem women.

Chapter 26

The Economics of Taxing Imports

It's relatively ugly. It's relatively slow. It's relatively unstable. It's relatively cramped inside. Nonetheless, there are hundreds of happy Volkswagen owners in countries other than Germany. Why have so many non-Germans decided to buy the VW instead of their own nationally-made cars. Any of you readers who have purchased a Volkswagen know the reason - in your own mind, it's a better deal than any domestic alternative. People buy foreign cars when they think they are getting a better deal by doing so. This is of course true in all voluntary transactions. People will only trade when there are gains to be made in the process; i.e. people will only transact business with other people voluntarily if both parties feel that they are made better off by the transaction. In the international economic sphere, the same is true. Nations will trade among themselves because there are gains to be had from such trading.

The amount of world trade has increased dramatically in the last 175 years. In 1800 it was a mere £600 million in terms of today's purchasing power. Just before the Depression, it reached almost £30 billion. The Great Depression slowed things down a bit, and that figure was not to be reached again until 1950. Today world trade averages in excess of £125 billion a year. If countries did not realize that they were all gaining from this increased world trade, it would not be growing at such a fast rate. After all, the transactions involved are, for the most part, voluntary, between individual citizens in different countries. Even though the argument in favour of world trade is a relatively simple one, it is difficult for some unions and industries to accept the declines in demand for their services or products that may come about as a result of increased world trade.

In order to understand why all nations can be made better off as a result of trade, we must distinguish between a nation's comparative advantage in the production of a good or service and a nation's absolute advantage in producing a wide variety of goods. Member countries of the EEC may have an absolute advantage in producing a wide variety of goods in the sense that they can produce those goods with fewer man-hours of labour. This does not mean that the EEC countries will not trade with other countries. On the contrary, the EEC countries benefit by specializing in only those endeavours in which they have a comparative advantage. An example of comparative advantage may clarify this statement.

America's William Howard Taft was perhaps the best stenographer in the world before he became President of the United States. He had an absolute advantage in stenography. When he became President, by definition, he also had an absolute advantage in being President. As President, he did not specialize in stenography even though he was the best. The advantage to him and to the nation of devoting all his time to being President was much greater than the loss of his stenographic output. His comparative advantage lay in presiding over that nation, not in taking dictation at 200 words per minute.

Any country may have an absolute advantage in the production of computers and roller skates, in the sense that it can produce both goods with fewer man-hours of labour than any other. However, it may let other countries produce roller skates for it because its comparative advantage lies in producing computers. The country gains from exchanging the computers it produces for the roller skates produced by other countries.

In general, people discover their own comparative advantage by contrasting the return from doing one job with the return from another one. An executive in a large corporation may have an absolute advantage in doing fifteen different tasks for that company. For example, he may be able to type better than all of the secretaries, wash windows better than any of the window washers, file better than any of the file clerks, and carry messages better than any of the messengers. His comparative advantage, however, lies in being an executive. He knows that his comparative advantage lies in this job because he is paid more for being an executive than he would be paid in any of those other jobs. The company willingly pays his salary as an executive because the value of his output in that job is at least as large as the salary paid him.

The key to understanding comparative advantage lies in the realization that total resources are fixed at any moment in time. An individual, a company, or a nation must decide how it will allocate its available resources at a given moment. No one can use a resource in two different jobs at the same time. Even if companies or nations are absolutely better at doing everything, they will still specialize in those tasks in which they have a comparative advantage, for in that specialization they maximize the return from the use of their time and resources.

Japan is a good example of how a nation can benefit from exploiting its comparative advantage and engaging in a large volume of world trade. Japan's recovery since World War II has been as miraculous as was Germany's. Real income in that country has been growing at an average rate of about 10 per cent a year. Foreign trade has grown at an even faster rate. While real income doubled between 1952 and 1960, for example, exports from Japan more than tripled. During the early sixties Japan's exports were doubling almost every five years. Japan has used its comparative advantage in manufacturing to expand its export markets in cameras, motor-cars, and, believe it or not, steel products. It is hard to imagine how a country without a resource base composed of the raw materials needed to make steel products can become a net exporter of them, but Japan's comparative advantage is in the machining of the steel and not in the exploitation of raw resources to make it; therefore, Japan imports iron ore and exports cold-rolled steel.

In spite of the obvious advantage to trade on an individual, intracountry, and international level, many statesmen, and workers as well, want to put tight import controls, or high import taxes, on all goods that compete with anything that is produced in any individual country.

More than two centuries ago the mercantilists had similar ideas about what was good for the nation. They felt that it was proper for a country to expand its exports without expanding its imports in order to acquire large amounts of gold; i.e. they felt that a trade surplus was the only way a nation could gain from trade. Of course, this notion ignores the concept of comparative advantage developed above. In the long run, exports have to equal imports. Countries do not ship goods to other countries and get nothing but pieces of paper in return; they will trade goods only for other goods.

The effects of import tariffs on the overall welfare of any economy can be analysed in a manner that quite readily points out the costs to society. The reader must be warned that as always, this so-called welfare cost analysis does not distinguish between who gains and who loses, in the sense that no special weight is attached to the gains or losses of one individual as opposed to another.

Let's consider the situation in which steel is produced in Britain and also imported into Britain. Suppose that Britain can purchase all the steel it wants, in the absence of tariffs, at the going world price of steel. United Kingdom producers are not technologically efficient enough to produce all the steel the British demand at the currently prevailing world price. United Kingdom producers can be induced to furnish more domestically produced steel only through an increase in the domestic price of steel. In the face of world competition, this is impossible without tariffs.

Now suppose that the British Government places a tariff on imported steel. The domestic price of steel can increase above the world price of steel, for anyone in the United Kingdom who wishes to purchase foreign steel must pay the before-tax world price plus the tariff. The Government obtains revenue from all the imports of steel into the United Kingdom. Now that the effective world price of steel is raised in the domestic economy, British producers of steel can profitably expand their production. They will have to bid resources away from other sectors of the economy, though. The increased production of steel necessitates a reduction of production somewhere else in the economy. Of course, now that domestic production of steel has increased, Britain will import less. Some resources were used in export producing sectors of the economy to produce the exports needed to exchange for imported steel. Since the imports of steel have been reduced, those resources used in producing exports to exchange for the imports are released to produce other goods. The fact remains, however, that Britain's given stock of resources will yield less steel by reallocating its production to the domestic steel industry. Britain could have acquired more steel with the same resources if it had left resources in the export producing sector and traded those exports for foreign steel. This is so because of Britain's **comparative advantage** in the production of the export goods.

What about the consumers of steel? When the domestic price of steel rises, less will be demanded by consumers. Manufacturers will use less steel and more substitutes for steel. They have an incentive at the higher domestic price of steel to develop production techniques which minimize the use of steel. As consumers of steel switch to substitutes which are produced domestically, some resources used to produce the exports needed to trade for imported steel will be released from those export industries. These resources can now be used to produce steel substitutes. However, the value of those steel substitutes produced will necessarily be less than the value of the imported steel those exports could have been traded for. If not, the resources would already have been used in steel-substitute production. The resources were in the export industry to begin with because they had a comparative advantage in the production of exports.

The payment of the tariff on the remaining imports of steel reduces the consumer surplus of steel consumers but this is not a part of the welfare loss, for the tax revenue can be returned to society in the form of a tax cut elsewhere.

Import tariffs, therefore, create welfare losses just like any other taxation of specific products does. Britain gets less from the use of its resources because the resources shift out of, say, export industries and into domestic production of steel or steel substitutes and thus are no longer being used in the areas in which they have a comparative advantage. People are faced with a set of prices that no longer reflects the social (world) costs of production. Consumers will purchase less steel than is socially optimal and producers in Britain will produce more steel than is socially optimal.

Individuals within the Common Market obviously are benefiting from the reduced import taxes paid on all goods shipped within Common Market countries. However, to the extent that the tariff wall which surrounds the Common Market exists, EEC consumers lose out. On net, it is not clear if they are actually better off because of the EEC's tariff policies.

Chapter 27

The Economics of Exchange Rates

For many years now, Common Market countries have discussed the notion of a common currency for a united Europe. On several occasions, there have been attempts to peg the value of each Common Market country's currency at some fixed rate with the others. And on several occasions, such price-fixing has fallen apart.

After World War II, there was talk about a dollar shortage. Starting in the 1950s, however, European countries found themselves with increasing supplies of United States dollars.

For a number of years, Germany was selling more products abroad than it was buying. The result was a continued export surplus.

The above problems are only several of the numerous ones that are associated with international finance. To understand the origins of current international monetary problems, we must go back in history to the gold standard which was in effect before the Depression and which has been desired for some time now on the part of a number of prominent European economists, in particular Jacques Ruffe in France.

Nations operating under the gold standard agreed to redeem their currency in gold when this was requested by any holder of that currency. While gold was not necessarily the means of exchange for world trade, it was the unit to which all currencies under the gold standard were pegged. Since all currencies in the system were linked to gold, exchange rates between those currencies were fixed.

Assume for the moment that there are no private purchases or sales of financial assets between citizens of different countries. Only goods and services are traded. Let's further assume that Sweden and Great Britain are the only two countries which trade with each other. If Swedes want to purchase British goods, they must convert their kronas into pounds. After all, British entrepreneurs want to be paid in pounds so that they can pay their workers. On the other hand, British citizens who want to buy Swedish goods must convert their pounds into kronas. The rate at which pounds can be converted into kronas is called the **exchange rate**. Under the gold standard, exchange rates were fixed because the values of currencies were linked to gold.

This fixed exchange rate system provided an adjustment mechanism that eliminated any excess supply or demand for currencies on the foreign exchange market at the fixed exchange rate. Suppose, for example, pounds are in excess supply on the foreign exchange market at the pegged exchange rate. The price level is too high in Britain. At the fixed exchange rate, British citizens desire to purchase 'too many' Swedish goods because they are cheap in comparison with British goods. Swedes, however, purchase 'too few' British goods because of their high price in comparison with Swedish goods. To prevent a devaluation of the pound, the British Government must be a residual buyer of pounds (seller of foreign currencies or gold). The increased supply of foreign currencies or gold and the increased demand for pounds (brought about by the purchases of pounds by the British Government) will eliminate the excess supply of pounds on the foreign exchange market. The exchange rate will remain at its fixed level. However, the sale of foreign currencies or gold by the British Government will reduce the stock of high-powered money in Great Britain just as would the sale of a bond in open market operations. The money supply in Great Britain will fall by a multiple of the contraction in the stock of high-powered money.

Consequently, under the fixed exchange rate rules, any country whose currency was in excess supply automatically experienced a reduction in its money supply. Such a fall in the money supply will reduce total spending in that country, reducing the demand for imports as well as the demand for domestic output. As the demand for imports falls, British citizens will supply fewer pounds to the foreign exchange market. The fall in British prices resulting from the reduction in total spending will induce Swedes to purchase more British goods at the fixed exchange rate, increasing the demand for pounds. Thus, the foreign exchange market will return to equilibrium with the supply and demand for pounds equal at the pegged exchange rate.

If pounds are in excess demand at the pegged exchange rate, the monetary authorities must be residual buyers of foreign currencies or gold and thus suppliers of pounds. Their aim is to prevent the pound from appreciating in terms of the krona. In the process of buying foreign currencies, the stock of high-powered money in Great Britain will expand, creating a multiple expansion of the money supply. The resulting increase in British prices and income will increase the supply of pounds and reduce the demand for pounds at'the fixed exchange rate, returning the foreign exchange market to equilibrium.

The essential feature of a truly fixed exchange rate system is that each country's monetary policy can no longer be controlled by the national central bank. The very act of purchasing or selling foreign exchange (currencies) to peg exchange rates produces a change in the money supply which returns the foreign exchange market to equilibrium. No country that submits to a truly fixed exchange rate discipline can have control over its money supply. The domestic price level must be determined by world prices. The domestic money supply reacts to purchases and sales of foreign exchange or gold to produce that price level.

During the 1930s central banks asserted their independence of the fixed exchange rate discipline. National central banks refused to allow an excess demand or supply of their currency in the foreign exchange markets to affect their own domestic money supplies. They were not going to give Balance of Payments problems priority over domestic economic considerations.

The impact of purchases or sales of foreign exchange on the stock of high-powered money oan be offset through open market operations. A country forced to sell foreign exchange to support its currency's value can purchase bonds in open market operations to insulate the money supply from foreign exchange stabilization operations. These **sterilization policies** (the use of open market operations to offset the impact of purchases or sales of foreign exchange on the stock of high-powered money) will prevent the foreign exchange market from returning to equilibrium. If the money supply is unaffected, there will be no change in total domestic spending and prices to correct the Balance of Payments deficit. Excess demand for foreign exchange will persist. Eventually the country will exhaust its supplies of foreign exchange to sell in support of its own currency, resulting in the currency's devaluation. These currency crises are the outcome of differing monetary policies among nations. If central banks permit their money supplies to adjust in response to foreign exchange stabilization policies, no such crises need occur.

Truly fixed exchange rates can be maintained only if national monetary policies are co-ordinated so as to produce the same rate of inflation in all countries whose currencies are pegged to each other. If countries insist on pursuing independent monetary policies, exchange rates must eventually be realigned to reflect differences in purchasing power among currencies.Monetary policies that fail to reflect stabilization operations in the foreign exchange market are the cause of Balance of Payments problems.

In the 1930s practically all countries in the world were in a very serious depression. Central banks were unwilling to have their money supplies and aggregate demand contract just because of a Balance of Payments deficit. This effectively destroyed the automatic mechanism by which equilibrium is restored in the foreign exchange market. We could not, therefore, expect a truly permanently fixed exchange rate system to last for ever. Virulent economic nationalism, born during the 1930s and surviving today, prevents most countries from allowing their money supplies to be dictated by the actions of people in other countries through the foreign exchange markets. Central banks today continue to be residual buyers and sellers of their own currency in times of Balance of Payments disequilibrium, but through their open market sales and purchases, they prevent changes in the money supply necessary to restore equilibrium. The mechanism which operated under the gold standard for bringing the foreign exchange market back into equilibrium has been effectively destroyed by sterilization operations.

The world is no longer on a pure gold standard, nor has it been for some time on a fixed exchange rate standard. Rather, the world has generally been experiencing a floating exchange rate system, although some governments have attempted to keep fixed exchange rates for their own currencies. Floating exchange rates permit the foreign exchange rate to return to equilibrium without any effect on the country's money supply. The exchange rate itself changes instead of the money supply. If countries do not peg exchange rates, supply and demand for currencies on the foreign exchange market will determine the exchange rate.

To illustrate the adjustment mechanism under a floating exchange rate system, let us return to our simplified world consisting of Sweden and Great Britain. The demand for Swedish goods by British citizens constitutes a supply of pounds to the foreign exchange market. The demand for pounds is derived from the demand for British goods by Swedes. If prices in Sweden rise by

10 per cent while prices in Great Britain remain constant, the exchange rate must change to produce equilibrium in the foreign exchange market. If exchange rates remained constant, Swedish goods would rise in price relative to British goods in both countries, pricing Swedish goods out of the world market. The Swedish inflation would reduce the supply of pounds to the foreign exchange market at the constant exchange rate because British citizens would buy fewer Swedish goods at the increased price. The demand for pounds would increase at the fixed exchange rate because Swedes would buy more British goods as the price of Swedish goods increased relative to the price of British goods. When the exchange rate is allowed to adjust to the changes in supply and demand, however, the pound will appreciate by 10 per cent in terms of the krona. In Sweden, Swedish goods will increase in price by 10 per cent, but so will the krona price of British goods, for it will take 10 per cent more kronas to purchase each pound. In Great Britain, the price of British goods will remain constant, but so will the pound price of Swedish goods, for it will take 10 per cent fewer pounds to purchase each krona.

If exchange rates are free to fluctuate in response to private supply and demand, each country can independently pursue its own monetary policy. Some countries may prefer high rates of monetary growth and inflation, while other countries maintain slower rates of monetary growth and price stability. Those countries with higher than average inflation rates will experience a devaluation of their currency relative to other currencies. No country's goods will be priced out of the world market through domestic inflation.

Germany has generally maintained a slower rate of monetary expansion and less inflation than have most countries of Western Europe and the United States. The German general index of wholesale prices was at the same level in 1969 as it was in 1964.

During that same time period general wholesale prices in the United States, for example, increased by over 12 per cent. As a result of these differing rates of inflation, Germany had continued to develop an export surplus. As world prices continued to rise at a faster rate than German prices, German goods became cheaper in comparison with non-German goods. German exports increased rapidly, but German imports were discouraged by the rapid increase in world prices at the fixed exchange rate. This trade surplus implies excess demand for deutschemarks. In order to maintain the fixed exchange rate, the West German Government has had to purchase foreign exchange (mainly United States dollars) and sell deutschemarks on the foreign exchange market. In November 1969, the West German Government finally stopped purchasing dollars and other foreign exchange. Immediately the deutschemark appreciated in value and eventually the West German Government re-pegged its value at the new exchange rate. As inflation continued in the United States, the West German Government again had to purchase large inflows of dollars to prevent the deutschemark from appreciating. Again in May 1971, the Germans stopped buying dollars and let the mark float up in value in comparison with the dollar. The recent history of the deutschemark illustrates the difficulties of maintaining fixed exchange rates in the absence of co-ordinated monetary policies. If countries have different monetary policies resulting in different rates of inflation, exchange rates must eventually be realigned. The rash of currency crises the world has experienced in the last decade are the ultimate consequence of independent monetary policies in a world of fixed exchange rates.

So long as the world remains mainly on a floating exchange rate standard, we can be reasonably assured that no more currency 'crises' will occur.

Chapter 28

The Economics of World Inflation

Today inflation in most industrial countries throughout the world is running at double the rates of the 1960s, and there has been an almost universal acceleration in the past few years. As everyone knows, when price levels rise, the purchasing power of money shrinks. In order to understand why it is that the pound, krona, deutschemark, gilder and franc buy so little today relative to what they used to buy in years past, it is necessary to look into the relationship between the amount of cash made available in any country and what people want to do with that cash.

The best way to understand the link between increases or decreases in the total amount of cash in a country, or the total money supply, the total aggregate economic activity is to look at what people use money for. Obviously, people hold money - i.e. currency and checking account balances - as a temporary method of maintaining purchasing power for future use. They also hold money to use it as a medium of exchange. Generally, though, people don't immediately cash their pay cheques and buy everything they need for the rest of the pay period. You and I keep some of our earnings in the form of checking account balances and currency in our wallets or purses. We have some level of desired money balances which turns out to be primarily a function of how large our income is. When our income rises, we end-up keeping bigger money balances. When our income goes down, we end-up keeping smaller money balances. There are variations from person to person, but as a general rule this relationship holds.

So it turns out that people's desire to hold money balances is mainly a function of their incomes. If the central bank in any one country suddenly injects a lot of cash into circulation, some people will have a larger money balance than they desire to hold. The only way for them to reduce their money balances is to spend more money than they usually do. When lots of people do likewise, aggregate demand increases. On the other hand, if the central bank in any country happens to take a lot of cash out of circulation, some people end-up with less money balances than they desire to hold. The only way they can increase the average number of pounds, for example, they have on hand is by spending less than they usually do. In this manner, aggregate demand is curtailed.

Now, in a growing economy with increases in productivity and population, the number of francs or pounds or kronas or gilders or deutschemarks, or what have you, that have to be put into circulation in order to simply maintain a stable price level, is probably 2 to 3 per cent of the current money stock per year. That means that the central bank should probably be injecting money into each nation's economy at the rate of 2 to 3, or maybe 4 per cent per year. When it does otherwise, it causes fluctuation in total aggregate demand, and that's just what the central banks have done ever since their existence. Monetary fine-tuning by the world's central banks has resulted in numerous ups and downs in economic activity with concommitant pains and joys of recessions and booms.

In fact, when a nation is at full employment, it just can't produce any more than it's already producing. Any excess demand has to translate itself into rising prices. That's what inflation is all about.

In fact, if we looked at all sustained periods of inflation in any country in the world, we find that the money supply has concurrently been growing at abnormally high rates. The relationship is most striking when we view excessive inflation, such as those which occur daily in Latin America and that which occurred as hyper-inflations in Hungary, Russia and East Germany. Students of inflation have come to realize that no sustained rise in prices in any nation on earth is possible without a sustained increase in the money supply.

It's an undeniable fact that when people want more of something than is available, they bid up the price. It's also undeniable that when there is more of something around that people want, they don't value it so highly. What is the value of your national currency to you? It's probably at least equal to what you can trade it for. So the money prices of things should reflect the value of your cash. If the supply of that cash goes up drastically, what you hold in the form of cash will certainly be worth less; i.e. you won't be able to trade your cash for as much stuff any more. And so, we have the rising cost of living.

You've probably heard that 'a little inflation is a good thing'. Don't believe a word of it. To say that a little steady inflation is a good thing because it promotes higher employment, buoyant spirits, and so on is to say that all businessmen are stupid and that all workers are terribly slow in realizing what's happening. It's hard to fool all of the people all the time. If the government printing presses cause prices to rise at 10 per cent a year, year in and year out, won't businessmen begin to expect the trend to continue? Won't syndicates begin to expect it also and demand wages that rise to cover the rising cost of living? Won't at least some non-union workers demand that they, too, get wage increases to cover the inflationary erosion of their pay cheques?

The evidence supports an affirmative answer to all those questions. In countries with steady, predicted inflation, all prices including those we call wages adjust step-by-step with the rising cost of living. This just tells you that you can't fool workers into working for falling *real* wages (money wages divided by the rising cost of living, or what you can really buy with your money), even though this could get rid of unemployment. With prices rising faster than wages, entrepreneurs find it more profitable to hire more workers so we have less unemployment.

But the only way for this to work is to fool everyone continuously by continually changing the rate of inflation in some unpredictable fashion. Many governments in the world today have done just this at times. Since the cost of living has risen sometimes at a fast rate, sometimes at a slow rate, nobody can adjust things completely. Since people were fooled, the economy suffered sometimes from over-heating, sometimes from under-heating.

How can you as individuals avoid the costs of unanticipated inflation in your own country? Well, it's not easy, but one particular method that has been used with great success in at least one country involves putting the entire economy, public and private sectors alike, on a price index escalator. We can see how it works by looking at what has happened in Brazil.

There, all contracts are written in real terms in the sense that they are tied to a price index with full and complete adjustments for both rises and falls in that price index. The same is true for interest rates of any kind and for the income tax brackets and personal exemptions that are allowed when paying taxes. All business accounting procedures have to be tied to the index to constantly ring out fictitious values of inventory and capital assets.

What happens is that every three months or so in Brazil, a monetary correction factor is announced by the Government. It is none other than an indication of the rate of inflation over the past three months. If you have a savings account and the monetary correction factor is, say, 2 per cent, then the principle in your savings account is increased by 2 per cent. So, too, are your wages and the value of any other contractual assets that you have. In this system, each worker is protected from inflation and would always be on an equal footing with any other worker in the economy, as well as with any entrepreneur. The Government is no longer able to benefit from inflation by having revenues rise simply through the workings of some sort of progressive tax schedules. The little man's savings are secured against inflation and essentially there are no distortions in the economy due to an inflation rate which jumps all over the place. More importantly, the central banks and the government officials in each country under a régime of complete and pervasive cost of living escalator clauses could affect in no way the workings of the economy through stabilization policies. Hence, there would be no excuse for governments to curtail the rate of inflation because there would be no short-run deleterious unemployment effects.

The idea may sound a little farfetched, but it has worked wonders in Brazil. Brazil has reduced its rate of inflation from over 100 per cent a year to about 15 per cent a year in a little over a decade without experiencing any increases in unemployment. Moreover, as it becomes increasingly more advantageous to negotiate cost of living escalator clauses in all contracts, they will in fact become a way of life. Inflation is only an evil if it cannot be anticipated by everyone. Once it is anticipated, or can be taken care of by writing all contracts essentially in real terms rather than in nominal or money terms, it will no longer be considered the number one economic problem in the world today.

Until we reach the time where it isn't considered the number one problem, we will continue to use stop-gap measures to try to slow it down, and one of the most popular is obviously wage and price controls, to which we now turn.

Chapter 29

The Economics of Price Controls

Price controls seem to be used as perennial political measures to combat ever-rising prices throughout the British Isles and on the Continent. In spite of the fact that the rate of inflation in all the countries of the world today is the highest it has been for most of them, the desire to impose mandatory limits on prices and wages continues to be a popular political football kicked around by numerous politicians, both actual and potential, and believed in by the vast majority of the public.

In 1973, the Swiss Parliament passed numerous Government measures to combat what it called 'economic over-heating'. The powers to supervize prices, including wages, profits, and dividends, were greatly extended. Up until 1973, the Swiss Government had consistently rejected the idea of a freeze, but starting in that year, the Government decided that if any prices rose 'unjustifiably', it would be forced to lower them and to subject subsequent increases to authorization.

The French Government has used price controls on numerous items, and every once in a while one reads in the newspapers that it has clamped a new set of price controls on a wider range of basic food and industrial goods in its bid to stem the country's galloping inflation. Belgium, Luxembourg, Holland, Denmark, Britain, Sweden, Finland, Norway, and the United States have all attempted in the past few years to control prices, but to no avail. As we saw in the last chapter, prices continue to rise in all of these countries. Indeed, the history of price controls is one of abysmal failure whenever they were applied in any effective way.

In the year 301, for example, Roman Emperor Diocletian issued a price control edict. He boldly fixed the maximum price at which beef, grain, eggs, clothing, and other articles should be sold and prescribed the penalty of death for anyone who disposed of his wares at a higher figure. There were also wage controls then.

Teachers, lawyers, physicians, bricklayers, tailors, and others could not demand a higher than prescribed salary. A Roman named Lactantius wrote in 314 that 'there was . . . much bloodshed upon very slight and trifling accounts; and the people brought provisions no more to market since they could not get a reasonable price for them'; and this increased the dearth so much that after many had died by it, the law itself was laid aside.'

The failure of price controls that time didn't stop Emperor Julian from imposing them on grain prices in the ancient city of Antioch sixty years later. He tried to roll prices back to a level which hadn't been seen for many years, except during those in which grain was in fact in plentiful supply. Historian Edward Gibbon maintains that the results were predictable and disastrous. Merchants grabbed-up corn released from the Imperial storehouse and withheld it from the market. The small quantities that appeared in Antioch were secretly sold at high illegal prices.

In the United States, the Continental Congress imposed price controls on colonial goods with equally disastrous effects. Farmers and producers refused to sell at the lower prices. Instead, they sold their wares to the British who were willing to pay reasonable rates. The troops at Valley Forge almost mutinied for this and other reasons.

Compare the situation in Germany after World War I and after World War II. In the first situation, there were no price controls; in the second situation, there were very effective ones. You'll remember that the Allies, using the Treaty of Versailles, had imposed immense reparation payments on that war-torn country after World War I. In order to finance these payments, the Weimar Republic printed marks - lots of them. By 1923 the German Government was spending 12 billion marks more than it was receiving in taxes. Its expenditures were seven times as great as its revenues. The mark-United States dollar exchange rate went from 14 to 1 in 1919 to 4,200,000,000 to 1 in 1923! However, there were no price controls so that prices and wages adjusted rapidly to the influx of marks. In the end, there were hourly changes in prices. A strange thing occurred, though. Output in post-World War I Germany did not fall until the last six months of that country's hyper-inflation. At that time, people got tired of pushing a wheelbarrow full of marks to the store just to buy a knockwurst. They finally resorted to barter.

In World War II, Nazi Germany controlled prices. So-called economic crimes, such as selling products above the maximum legal price, were immediately dealt with in a very harsh manner. When the Allies occupied Germany after the war, they didn't dismantle the rationing scheme, though they did soften the punishment somewhat. It was felt that pandemonium would have broken out in an already chaotic situation. For three years, strict price controls remained in effect. But something very strange was happening. The number of marks in circulation increased a phenomenal 400 per cent during that period, while output fell by 50 per cent. The mark became useless for obtaining goods and services because of widespread shortages at the controlled prices. Price controls in occupied Germany were extremely successful. They were so successful that the official price index hardly budged at all. But what they did essentially was to destroy the monetary standard in that country. People in post-World War II Germany could not get any goods for their deutschemarks.

The juxtaposition of these periods in German history demonstrates what can happen during periods of phenomenal increases in the amount of money in circulation - with and without price controls.

If the money supply increases rapidly, the public's attempts to get rid of excess money balances produces excess demand for goods and services. Market prices will rise until people no longer want to decrease their average currency and checking account balances. If price controls prevent prices from rising, the excess demand for goods and services becomes apparent as shortages develop. At the legal price level, the demand for goods will exceed the supply of goods, requiring an alternative method of rationing the available supply. After all, individuals hold money balances in order to have a liquid stock of purchasing power over goods and services. If there are widespread shortages due to excess demand for goods and services, money no longer serves as a liquid stock of purchasing power over goods and services. Money balances can no longer perform the services for which they were held. The resort to barter or the creation of a new commodity currency, such as cigarettes, naturally follows.

A good contemporary example is in South America. When Chile's former (and late) Marxist President Allende simultaneously raised wages and froze prices in one stroke of his governmental pen, appliance stores were empty within a short time. Chileans didn't want to keep the increased cash they ended up with, so they quickly went on a spending spree. Since prices could not rise in response, the spree stopped when stocks of goods were depleted.

In post-World War II Germany there essentially was a complete destruction of the monetary standard because people couldn't get any goods with their money. After price controls were lifted, a new banking system was instituted and the Marshall Plan became established. West Germany then experienced what has been called a miracle. Between 1948 and 1964 industrial production increased *600 per cent!* Real GNP tripled between 1950 and 1964. *Per capita* GNP in real terms increased faster in West Germany than in any other Western European or North American country. Of course, this experience was a 'miracle' only to those who were not initiated into the mysteries of economics. Astute readers know the real cause.

America also used price controls during World War II, as it already had done to some extent during World War I. However, they were much more extensive during World War II and people now point out how successful they were. That may or may not be true. What certainly is true is that it was a hard job being a price-controller. In a *Playboy* interview some years ago, Professor John Kenneth Galbraith of Harvard University related his experience with the United States Office of Price Administration during World War II. At one point in the interview, Dr Galbraith said he had decided, during one trying moment in those war-torn years, that it might be easier for a price of $5 to be set on everything. Such a radical idea is proof enough that the job of keeping a lid on prices during World War II could not have been easy.

What's important to remember about World War II price controls is that: (1) they occurred during a period of wartime patriotism; and (2) they were administered by about 400,000 paid and volunteer price observers scattered around the country. You also have to remember that black and grey markets were rampant during World War II. It is not clear what the true price index actually was during that period, for the official one only took account of published prices, not transactions prices. The same is true for the official price index today in the United States. What does it mean to say that prices rose only 5 per cent a year when, during the last few years, there were numerous products you couldn't get at any price because producers had stopped producing them? Do you want to put a price of infinity on those products and put that into your price index? It then becomes very large indeed, right?

What never seems to be understood about price controls is that they're only effective so long as there's no reason for prices to rise anyway. As soon as there is a reason for prices to rise, they either become ineffective because people cheat, or if they are in fact strictly enforced, they become destructive, as we have all found out. Why do they become destructive? Simply because at a price set less than one which doesn't create a shortage, consumers who can get a product at all at that price don't have an incentive to conserve the product in question, and producers don't have enough incentive to increase production. Everybody agrees that if the price of petrol went to £2 a gallon, people would use less. Everybody also agrees that if the price of petrol went to £2 a gallon, producers would have an added profit incentive to increase refining capacity, to tap new wells, to increase capacity utilization of existing equipment, etc.

The important element in this whole discussion is not so much the specific points that have been made. Rather, what is important is your increased awareness of the futility of trying to block natural economic forces in your country or in the world. What governments say they can do and what they say they are doing do not necessarily correspond with what is actually happening. Delve into the issues a little more deeply when a news commentator or a government official tells you that a crisis is upon the land and the only thing we can do is this, that, or the other thing. Don't automatically agree. If you do, you may be sorry, just as those of us who listened and believed politicians and the media over the past few years are certainly sorry we were so naive.